I0087626

Your Journey to Happiness

TRADE YOUR WORRIES AND REGRET FOR YOUR HAPPILY EVER AFTER

By: Gina Colvario Krupka, CLC

Copyright © 2013 Gina Colvario Krupka, CLC
Believe In You Today Publications

All Rights Reserved.

ISBN-10: 0615742173
ISBN-13: 9780615742175

Table of Contents

My Inspiration

This book was conceived in the midst of the most devastating time in my life. Diane, my only sibling and best friend, had just been diagnosed with stage four lung cancer. Two weeks after Diane was diagnosed, my father was also diagnosed with stage four colon cancer. My father had surgery right away and my sister had been given every treatment known to modern medicine.

I had just been laid off and was commuting two states away several times per week to help care for Diane and my 9 and 11 year old nephews. I was beyond distraught. How could this be happening, yet it was. In the midst of the chaos and fear, I clearly remember having moments of being present and knowing in that moment I was and would make it through. There were moments I noticed although my world seemed to be crumbling around me, I could and would still feel joy. I even asked a friend if I was delirious to seem okay through such suffering.

Even through my darkest times, there was still good in the world. That awareness was the seed of this book. As with many lessons, this was learned through trials, grief and loss.

Today I realize that, while these lessons may be opportunities for growth, they do not always make you stronger. My sister's death two months after her diagnosis, my father's four subsequent surgeries and then my mother being diagnosed with stage four cancer in her pancreas all within a year, taught me that getting through difficult times may be automatic. The question of how much each changes us is to be determined by each individual. Every event within our life changes us. The question is "how much?"

Experience is the hardest road to growth. Often we will have similar hardships in life until we learn the lesson and react differently. We are creatures of habit by nature and although it is insanity to repeat the same behavior, while expecting different results, often that is exactly what we do.

There are many methods of learning. We can also learn by other's example. We can take from the awe of nature. We can see the big picture in life and decide what place in it we would like to occupy today. If we are not consciously creating, it will be done for us subconsciously. Whatever we focus our attention on with emotion we create or draw to us.

It took me a while to get myself refocused. I still feel the aftershocks of the emotions from my sister's death. I experience waves of sadness and disbelief, but I use it to push myself to accomplish all the things Diane never could. I know she was and is still proud of me and would want her death to be a catalyst toward my self-realization, rather than to be used as an excuse to never achieve my dreams.

Every day we get to direct the winds of change; our attitudes are our sails that will take us where we want to go or will allow us to be lost at sea. Each event is an opportunity or a distraction. You get to chart your course to the greatness which lies within you. What is your life's purpose? What gifts do you offer the world in a way no other can? Each of us creates our course. Now that you know you have the choice, what direction do you choose?

If you are reading this book, then perhaps your chosen destination is happiness. As you live your life's purpose, you cannot help to share your light and joy with the world. If you are not happy, you are off track. Come with me as we chart a new course and adjust your sails. Your only requirement is an open mind and the willingness to feel joy. You deserve to be happy. You deserve to share your gifts and greatness with the world. Through your honesty and effort, you will find your clarity, truth and passion. You will find your way back to the greatness for which you were born.

Introduction

If the best things in life are free, how is it that so many miss them? These "things" cannot be bought or sold. They are priceless, and yet cannot be measured. We are born with all we need, yet we usually spend a lifetime in pursuit of these treasures.

We live in a society of bigger, better, faster and more. We search for the perfect spouse, car, job, home and lifestyle. We set monetary goals for the things we think we want; continuously seeking externally for the fleeting ring of glory- lasting contentment.

This book is a roadmap to happiness. Happiness is defined by Merriam-Webster's as: *"a state of well-being and contentment."* It is a state of feeling good, regardless of possession and circumstances. It is a **feeling**, not a destination.

Although at times it may seem fleeting, there is no need for it to be. We often seek it through external fixes. Many use fixes such as drugs, gambling, food, work, shopping or sex; just to name a few. They once brought us joy, although fleeting, and we wanted more. But no matter how much we get, we will never be fulfilled. We try to fill the internal hole of suffering, fear and anxiety with tangible distractions.

The problems are still there and progressively get worse, as we try to cover up and deny our lack. It felt good, so we seek that bliss. We take greater amounts and we feel less desired effects. This is the source of addiction; a separation, a disconnection from our Truth.

Addiction is one of the greatest distractions from true happiness. It creates weakness and insecurity. It causes obsession and disempowerment. Although the demon of addiction is internal, few deny its existence. It is not about weakness, but misdirection of power. It is a deep feeling of powerlessness that most people can relate to on some level.

Another great cause of pain is anger and resentment. Regardless of what others do, how you react to those actions determines its effects on you. Continuing to harbor negative thoughts and feelings poisons the keeper. Many people are giving away their power and strength unconsciously through fear.

Love is the feeling of true bliss, which is perfect joy. It always exists, but in the presence of fear, it is hidden. By honestly appraising your life today and our emotions around our current circumstances, you can determine the greatest needs for forgiveness, growth and healing.

The only path to true lasting happiness is well being. This book provides ten steps to tap into and maintain the flow of your personal well being. These steps will help you recognize what is truly important to you, so you can better appreciate yourself and your life today. It is time to acknowledge the power within you to no longer be overwhelmed, but empowered, enlightened and inspired. Well-being is an amazing regenerating source that can never be taken from you. It teaches us how to live in joy, regardless of external circumstances.

Happiness is your birthright! You can choose what you think about and focus your attention upon. You decide how you spend your time. You have the ability to feel joy in any moment. It is time to make the decision to be and stay happy. You choose what you think about and focus your attention on either consciously or subconsciously. You decide how you spend your time. You have the ability to be happy in any moment. So, it is time to make the decision to be and stay happy.

This book is set up to help you begin your journey. Wherever you may be starting from, THIS MOMENT is your starting point! All of your power is NOW! Your past experiences were only there to help you appreciate where you are going. There is no point in obsessing about your past or future. I often say, "the past is gone, the future will always be out of reach, but today is a gift; that is why it is called the present."

It is time to appreciate this gift to the fullest. You are meant for greatness. The only way to realize your full potential and purpose is to tap into your internal GPS, your intuition. This is not hard work; on the contrary, you already know what feels good. The challenge is to trust your emotions. Focus more on what you want, than what you do not want. That is the starting point for all. Choose a thought that makes you feel better. Feel good now! Continue to practice this in every moment. You do not have to be perfect to be happy, you simply need to start and then do the next right thing.

This process is not through escape, but by being present in this moment. To be calm, even in the midst of chaos. You can learn how to be steady in the midst of possibility. This moment of awareness is everything. Many are lonely in a crowd and stagnant in the midst of constant tasks. It is time to recognize what is most important in this moment. It is time to realize that in this moment: you do enough, you are enough and you have all you need. The beauty and power of life and all of its infinite possibilities are only available in the NOW!

As you go through these chapters, I invite you to see this book as much more than a list of facts. It is not just a book to read and think about. Take the time to journal on each question. Your path to joy will take incredible self-discovery. Each personal revelation will help to keep you directed toward your purpose and well being; together they are the steadfast to maintaining lasting happiness.

I also encourage you to utilize *Your Journal to Happiness*, the journal I wrote to accompany this process and take five minutes per day to help keep you on your path of awareness and joy.

Life is a miracle, not a struggle. Happiness is your purpose. Live in celebration as possibility blooms into opportunity. Either through a new beginning or at the end of a bad day, may these words help you find or return you to your path on *Your Journey to Happiness!*

CHAPTER I

Who are you?

Many people will answer this question too quickly. They assume it is asking about their station in life or how they are viewed by others. You must go deeper than age, stature, parent, child, gender, ethnicity or even vocation. In the quiet moments between the busyness of life, who are you?

- What matters most to you?
- What type of person are you?
- What are your values?
- How would your best friend describe why they appreciate you?
- How do you treat people?
- What is your attitude and temperament?
- Are you empowered and enthusiastic or frustrated and complacent?
- What makes you, YOU?

I realize that is a lot to think about, but that is what I am asking. If you do not know yourself, you cannot value yourself. You may not know how to change the patterns that no longer serve you or which ones you want to preserve and appreciate, but you can learn how to differentiate and adapt.

Much of whom you are, your personality, is developed in early childhood. Your influences such as parents, teachers, family and friends have helped to create your thought patterns, actions and reactions to life. The surroundings and circumstances with which you were raised, such as: heritage, financial status, education level, religion, relationships, communication style and traditions are a big part of who we are and can often subconsciously limit or enhance what you become. If you were encouraged and supported as a child, you would be more likely to take risks and believe in yourself. If you were given strictly negative attention, such as: being told you are useless or no good, not as smart as your brother or pretty as your sister, then you are less likely to have self-confidence. How could anybody like a person such as that? These sentiments, either spoken or implied, create layers of fear and insecurity. These people have a much lower chance of success, unless they consciously change their thoughts and self-talk. Self-talk is the inner voice that either says "yes I can" or "why bother, you will only be disappointed again." It can either serve you as affirmations and bring you strength or weaken you through your old tapes of the people who put you down or through your own fears and insecurities. You must listen to your thoughts and watch your actions and reactions consciously.

Step #1

Start where you are.

To begin on your journey, you must get to know yourself better. Know who you truly are, what your likes, dislikes, attributes and motivations are. It is not selfish to spend time on yourself, it is imperative! Without knowing yourself, you are unconsciously sharing only a part of yourself with the world; you are disconnected from your spirit of self or soul. This disconnect is often where we get off the track of joy.

I spent years in quiet desperation not knowing why or how to get out. The world saw a smile, but inside I was sad and alone. I knew at 16 years old that my passion was to teach and inspire others; but insecurities around my weight, stopped me from believing I had anything to offer. Separation from my life purpose kept me isolated and miserable. It took me years of soul searching through journaling, 12-step program work, reading books, spiritual studies and practices as well as attending many workshops and classes to realize that the source of my unhappiness was my disconnect from Spirit. I was living unconsciously as a victim to circumstance. I was not a conscious creator in my life.

For this book, you will need a journal. The questions in this book are not simply to think about, but you must write about each. In a quiet space, take some time thoroughly answering the many questions. Give them the care and attention you would give when nurturing a small child. You are your inner child. Connect to the inner part of you that often gets pushed aside. You may answer some questions easily and others you may find to be very difficult. What is most important is to answer them all honestly, lovingly and without judgment.

Relax into each and understand each questions intent and importance. The more difficult it is to write about, the greater the need to examine the source of the discomfort.

- What makes you happy?
- When was the last time you felt truly happy?
- What activities do you enjoy?
- When was the last time you planned and spent a day just for you?
- What did or would you do if you could spend a day any way you choose?
- When was the last time you were in awe of nature?
- When was the last time you watched the sun rise or set?
- When was the last time you truly felt excited about life?
- What is most important to you?
- What seems to be missing in your life?
- When was the last time you felt inspired?
- What is your life's purpose?

How did you get to be who and where you are today?

Your outlook on life, your character, is personality in motion. All of your traits and habits come together into your attitude. It is shown to the world by your actions and reactions to people and events. It is your personal expectation of life. If it is miserable or sarcastic, your experiences in life will be the same. The optimist, who sees the glass as half full, has more to appreciate and therefore more joy. Remember, your thoughts attract. Are you attracting more gratitude or more problems?

Many people have had a lifetime of self-defeat. They have spent years underachieving with low self esteem or over achieving with a low self-worth. You attract only what you feel you are worth. If you are a caretaker and accept great responsibility for others, they will usually allow you to take it on with little appreciation for what you do for them. Eventually, your over commitment becomes the expectation and they may even resent you doing less. If you act like a victim, people will view you as weak. People will treat you as well or poorly as you allow them to. It takes great self-knowledge and self-respect to establish healthy boundaries.

How you present and carry yourself speaks volumes to the world. Often appearances are stereotyped sub-consciously. Although we repeat the same patterns, we wonder why our life does not improve. Insanity is repeating the same action, but expecting different results.

Have you ever noticed people who go from one bad relationship to the next? People will say "they sure know how to pick them." The common denominator in the string of bad relationships is the same person choosing the same relationship with different people.

Another example is a person that hates their job and eventually leaves that job, whether they blame the boss, their pay or working conditions. Before long, they are unhappy in their new job as well. It may be a new location, but their patterns and choices have not changed. The person they present to the world went with them and they are often as unhappy as they were before. We have all heard the expressions "same old story" or "same stuff, different day." These are self-fulfilling prophecies. **If you do not change your habitual negative thought patterns and actions, the past is destined to repeat.** That is why so many people that win the lottery end up broke again. They may have won money, but they maintained a poverty mentality. Therefore, they were destined to return to that poverty they focused upon. **You must change the story you tell yourself in order to see lasting change.** It really is that simple. I did not say it was easy, but it is simple.

You may be upset reading this. You may be angry at the implications that you created your own bad breaks. I know it upset me when I realized I did this. I created my relationships, I chose my jobs, I overcommitted and underappreciated myself. I feared lack and focused upon lack, so lack kept showing up. It frustrated me to know that I held myself back for decades! Yes, how we were raised helped develop our personalities, but, if you are reading this now, you no longer have to accept ignorance as an excuse.

It is very important to understand this lesson without placing any judgment on ourselves or the people in our lives. Guilt serves no purpose! It will only hinder your growth. At this point forgive yourself and the people in your life. They did the best they could with the limited awareness they had at the time. Blame and shame are as useless as the tool of denial. If you want a different outcome, you must think and act differently. Release the shackles of past disappointments, trauma and loss. Let go of past hurts and insecurities. You too did the best you could with the knowledge you had.

Forgiveness

In many instances forgiveness is not easy. Anger and resentment are the poison we drink and expect the other to die. They eat away at your joy daily. Regardless of the circumstance or injustice, you must forgive. All forgiveness really is self-forgiveness. It is for the keeper, not the one it is held against. It is not approving of the action, but releasing the pain around it. It is not allowing that person back in to hurt you again, but realizing that every day you held that pain, you allowed them to do just that. You allowed them to resonate within your consciousness, which blocked your light and peace. In many cases the "dis-ease" caused illness and years of suffering.

I realize this is not an easy step for most people to take, but it is imperative if you want to take control of your life. To remain happy, you cannot give away your power to a past hurt. It has passed. Allow it to be done. Accept the event, not approve of it, but accept it and release it. Pain will happen in life, but suffering is optional. Suffering is staying in the pain without moving through it.

Grief and Loss

Sometimes you may not know how or may not want to forgive. Sometimes a loss will be so great that it takes a piece of us with it. I used to believe "that which does not kill us makes us stronger." I thought that until in one year my mother, father and sister were each diagnosed with stage four cancer and my only sibling was gone in two months with two young boys left behind. That year I also had two court custody battles, lost a job to a company closing, our family run store went out of business and my home was in foreclosure.

Now I say this not to relive my pain or to glorify my story; if anything it is humbling to write. Many people have had much worse; but that was my bottom. I realized then that getting through was automatic. I got up each morning and time passed, but I would never be the same. I share this because through it all I lived by some simple truths.

Simple Truths about Loss

1. Life is not fair. Some people will have more losses and pain than others.

2. You did nothing wrong to deserve this, it just is.

3. You will hurt sometimes. Do not try to avoid it, run from it, deny it or cover it up. Feel it and get through it or it never leaves. It will dull the joy in every experience until you do.

4. This too shall pass, **if** you allow it to.

5. Regardless of how life may change, it can still be wonderful.

6. Your spiritual connection with your Creator can and will help you through if you trust and allow it to.

Sometimes we need help with forgiveness, loss and moving forward in life. There are therapists, counselors, clergy, classes, workshops, books and many other tools that can help you through the hurt. Do not expect to have all of the answers. We all need help sometimes. It takes great strength to admit when you need help. It is weakness to remain stuck due to false pride.

Events and circumstances tint the glasses that you view life through. I feel much of my youthful innocence was lost to grief. I do not think that I will ever be the same. My life is wonderful, but different. I chose to move through the pain and help people in similar circumstances. I feel by using that pain and transmuting it into a loving message, it helps me find peace and understanding from it. I can see some good come from it. Am I stronger on the other side of pain? I do not know, but I realize my strength more than I ever had before.

If there is a muscle you never use, you will never know its capacity. Granted, there are some muscles that I wish I never needed.

The gift in awareness is that if you assimilate it, we never need to repeat a limiting pattern again. That is GREAT news! Life is wide open before you with a fresh canvas to color as you choose. What will you choose?

Step #2
Realize that you deserve to be happy.

"Our deepest fear is not that we are inadequate. Our deepest fear is that we are powerful beyond measure. It is our light, not our darkness that most frightens us. We ask ourselves, who am I to be brilliant, gorgeous, talented, fabulous? Actually, who are you not to be? You are a child of God. Your playing small does not serve the world. There is nothing enlightened about shrinking so that other people won't feel insecure around you. We are all meant to shine, as children do. We were born to make manifest the glory of God that is within us. It's not just in some of us; it's in everyone. And as we let our own light shine, we unconsciously give other people permission to do the same. °As we are liberated from our own fear, our presence automatically liberates others."

- Marianne Williamson from <u>A Return To Love</u>

These questions are designed to make you think about yourself. Understand that self-care is not selfish, but mandatory for a healthy life. When there is somebody in your life that you love, you give to them in time, attention, kind words, good deeds, gifts and you may even send them prayers. I am now asking you to care for yourself in the same way. **If you do not deem yourself worthy of your own attention, how or why would anyone else?**

There is a difference in overindulgence or arrogance. Nobody is any better than any other, but no worse either. We are all infinite possibility born of the Divine at birth. We each have incredible capacity for love, success and abundance in all areas of life. Only you can accept your good. Are you allowing it to flow to and through you? After all, the more you have, the more you have to offer, share and circulate all you have to offer with those you love and the world. It is not selfish to expect beautiful things and blessings; it is your birthright. Your Creator deemed you worthy. Selfishness is limiting your good and playing small. It serves nobody, especially God. You were created to be magnificent!

Are you shining?

Now this is what I believe to be the true difference between nature and nurture. You get to now think differently than many were taught. You can choose what you believe. **From this moment forward, all limits are self imposed.**

Why not you? Why not now?

Regardless of your current circumstances, you can be, do or have anything you believe you can. Your current life is a picture of your past thoughts and beliefs. Your future is based upon what you think and do today. So what will you choose? Will it be different or the same story played over in a different day? Again, to live a different life, you must be and act differently. If you are having difficulty with this concept, find a life coach or a metaphysician to help you realize that your reality is self imposed. **You are the designer of your life by the thoughts and beliefs you hold about it. If they are not working, change them!**

This may seem a radical thought to you, but it is no more farfetched than to believe you were created for mediocrity. You were born with the same physical and mental attributes as any other. All humans have a fraction of one percent difference in our DNA, yet some thrive while others simply survive. The difference is the desire and expectation behind it. This may seem like a crazy concept, but what do you have to lose? You determine your worth mentally, so when you look at your life today (relationships, job, finances and health) are you satisfied? I am not asking if you are grateful for your blessings, which is a different question altogether. Appreciation leads to more to be grateful for. I am asking if you may have sold yourself short. Is there more good waiting for you in life than you have been ready to allow in. The short answer is **YES!** There is always more good, because good is never finite. Take a minute to wrap your head around the fact that your good could never rob or deplete anybody else's good. Your perfect health could never take away from somebody else's health. Your wisdom and inspiration never takes a glimpse of it away from any other's wisdom or inspiration, if anything it encourages and helps others. No other ever needs to fail so that you can succeed. Even your financial prosperity only stands to benefit all that you circulate it to and through. Your good, if left unclaimed, is simply wasted.

I have given you a lot of responsibility for your life. For some, it will bring up anger; those are the victims who feel that they were wronged and given this life of mediocrity. Others will feel guilty, because it is just another thing that they did not do correctly. **Please understand that you could not know what you were never taught.** Let yourself off the hook and realize you simply did not know. But in your not knowing, you searched for Truth. In your quest for happiness, you were guided to this book and you took the chance and read it and now you know! You no longer need to wait for what others hand you. You no longer have to settle in life. You are no longer a victim of circumstance, predestined for plight. No, now you are a conscious co-creator in your life. It is as simple as cause and effect. Your belief and true expectation is the cause and your life and all that manifests from it is the effect.

I am not so arrogant to think that many of the people reading this have not already understood these concepts, after all, like often attracts like. I am very grateful for the multitudes of authors, speakers and teachers I have had that helped me come to my Truth. I do know, however, that we all need reminders from time to time. I had a friend Eddie that used to say he had a "built-in forgetter". It was like a bucket that starts full, but as circumstances come up in life, it gets holes poked in it and sometimes we forget. Yes, you are, as the rest of us are terminally human. Do not expect to be perfect, just do the best you can at the next right thing and make adjustments as you go. Life is meant to be enjoyed not picked apart critically. The more you critically pick apart your life, the less you will feel worthy of your good. Trust that everything happens for a reason. You need not understand or even like the reasons that have lead up to this moment, but appreciate those lessons and lovingly release them. Remember that judgment of any kind is always a detriment. Discernment and judgment are two different things. Discernment happens through understanding and loving eyes. Learn, but do not scorn.

There are many people bound up by guilt. As stated previously, guilt will never serve you! It is time to release the power of the past in order to allow the true power of now. For years, I was truly my own worst enemy. I too lived in the desolate land of the "shoulds, woulds and coulds." Today I often remind myself that I am enough, I do enough and have all I need just for this day. There is so much power in that statement! It is one of my daily affirmations; a practice and gift from the teachings of Louise L. Hay, a magnificent teacher and example of allowing greatness to unfold. She had an awful childhood and a difficult adulthood, yet continues to realize her infinite possibility. She even cured herself of cancer without surgery or modern medical treatment! Her book, _You Can Heal Your Life,_ talks about practical ways to change your thinking and life. I saw her speak last year, at 85 years of age. Her enthusiasm and love for life is electric and I believe the greatest reason for her personal achievement and success. She inspires me beyond words. Find people that inspire you to greatness. There are plenty of people that will try to tell you why you cannot do something, simply because they have not? Focus upon the people who are where you want to be, not just monetarily or in stature, but in the peace and joy they bring to all they do. Not for what they have, but who they are. **Remember, to have different, you must be different.**

CHAPTER 2

What do you really want?

There are two parts to your life, internal and external. To live in lasting happiness, you must explore both. The world sees the external part of you, but it is a result of the internal part of you.

Internal Reality

Internal reality drives your life, determines your worth and how you allow others to treat you. It also includes the spiritual and emotional aspects of self. Although both are dependent on your external life; both reciprocally depend upon each other.

The 3 most important self's

1. **Self esteem-** What you think of you is extremely important in all you do. Yours is the only opinion that matters. **What other people think of you is none of your business.** This does not give you the right to be disrespectful, but it allows you to value yourself regardless of any other point of view. There will always be people who will disagree with you, but that is not your stuff, it is theirs. Your part is to do the best you can in this moment. Be kind and loving, but not people

pleasing. There is a big difference. Your greatest good is not about them. If this area is lacking, your joy will always be diminished, because you may feel unworthy.

2. **Self-care-** This is not optional! It is mandatory for your well being. You must nurture your body, mind and soul. **You must give from the overflow, not your source,** which is why many caretakers live feeling depleted. You must sleep, eat, exercise, pray, meditate, daydream, vacation, have hobbies and still your body and mind. These activities replenish the energy that you give out to the world. If you do not take the time to refill yourself, you will have little to give. Living depleted is the greatest source of stress in life. It leads to feeling overwhelmed; which I will discuss later in greater detail. There are many ways to replenish your energy, but self-care is the fuel in your engine. It is what determines your level of performance and quality of life.

3. **Self-love-** Realize you are perfectly unique. There is not another individual just like you. Your body image and appreciation for your strength determine who you are, your self-worth. Many were disparaged by others or you may have been by comparing your insides to other people's outsides. Every person is a piece of this grand puzzle of life. Every puzzle piece is just as important and no two pieces are alike. If one piece of a puzzle is missing, the puzzle is incomplete. You must simply be your piece, not base your importance on color, shape or placement. **Appreciate your piece; it is the only way to be at peace within yourself.** Love you as you would love any child. You too are perfect. You were born that way. The only thing to be revealed is your appreciation

for your perfection. Accepting and appreciating who you are brings strength and will make you shine. That is what the world needs from you far more than money or a particular sized waist line. Yes, all are works in progress, but to be happy you must love and nurture yourselves enough to blossom.

When you have the three selfs, you will be better able to deal with life on life's terms. It is a great beginning step toward living consciously. They will give you the internal fortitude which strengthens your spirit, which is the personality and exuberance you share with the world. Only when you truly know, care for and appreciate yourself can you fully realize your purpose and live to your potential. That is what lasting happiness is made of, knowing and living what you love for the highest purpose. These are all steps toward self-realization.

Most people are not aware of their life purpose. Can you imagine deciding to write a book without a story or a theme? The book would simply ramble on in many directions and it would accomplish nothing. Yet, many people live their entire life that way. If you take the time to plan a vacation, why would you not put some planning into the direction of your life? If you feel stuck or see the same patterns repeating, do something different. Find a life coach, a mentor or if you know somebody living a life that seems to be fulfilled and ask them how they did it.

Remember, we all think and act differently. Your best thinking got you where you are today. Now be careful, that is an observation, not a judgment. It is important to realize you do not need to be perfect at anything, but being YOU. There will be times that you will need to ask for help. This too builds character differently than struggling through. I have come to believe that if I am stagnant or struggling, I am usually headed in the wrong direction. When you are following your bliss, life flows. It is work, but most often feels effortless. Struggle happens when I am fighting for my way, not allowing the highest or best way. Water always finds the most direct way down stream, trust the nature of life and go with the flow you are Divinely directed to. Trust that the next right thing will always appear.

External Reality

This is what the world sees, your relationships, lifestyle, career and attitude. We live in a society of bigger, better, faster and more. We are told external things that can be bought can bring happiness. They falsely promise fulfillment, but often only cause a greater void or separation from what matters most. Studies have proven the happiest people on this planet come from the poorest countries. Quality of life must be based on joy, not material possessions. Some of the happiest and most wonderful people I have ever known lived by meager means, while some of the wealthiest people I have known were miserable. Money is by no means a determining factor to joy. Yes, you can buy things that will bring temporary happiness. True fulfillment, which is lasting happiness and the realization of your purpose or dharma, only comes from within. The best things in life are free, but not always easily attainable if you live in a society that only validates the tangible.

How did our Western society get so turned around? When did we turn "family values" into a sound bite, not our ethics? Why would we be taught that financial status and having the bigger house, car or job is better, when it often takes more time away from what truly matters in life? When did we become consumers, not individuals? How do you stand a chance at lasting joy in a society where even on marriage is not sacred. The United States has over a 50% divorce rate with fewer people choosing to get married every year.

No, I am not getting negative; I am explaining how and why our default is toward material things. It is ingrained in us as children, if we are good, Santa Clause will bring us all we ask for. We are in the midst of a generation of soccer moms running their children around and picking up drive-thru take out for dinner because there is no time to prepare a meal, come together and eat. Society has changed. I do not write this in judgment, but simply want to point out that it is more important than ever in history to consciously spend your time and energy. Consciously choose your thoughts and actions or they may often become overwhelming. Realize that each moment is filled with choice, not expectations.

There is no quick fix. This is where escapism and addiction comes in. When you try to buy joy with temporary fixes, it only causes the hole you were trying to fill to grow deeper. It is time to take and maintain control of your life, attitude and well-being. This book is designed to help you return to your path of Truth whenever your emotions tell you that you are off course. The simple rule is that if you are unhappy, it is time to figure out why and make some adjustments. That does not mean end a relationship or leave a job, at least not usually. You are the reason you are happy or not, it is not the job or the marriage. You created your life. The circumstances are simply the manifestations of your beliefs or actions. If you do not determine the source of the discord, you are likely to fall into the same situations with different players. Geographical cures are never the answer, they just prolong the search. All understanding must come from within.

Without judgment or guilt ask yourself: what is it in me that helped create this aspect of my life? When you determine that, then you can make an educated decision. Change is only positive when it is for the better. Simply being different is just a distraction and there is plenty of that around. Again, you could not know what you were never taught. You are learning how to choose differently and should appreciate your growth.

Step #3
Believe in Yourself!

*"Whether you think you can,
or you think you can't - you're right."*

- <u>Henry Ford</u>

Your thoughts become things. Thoughts are your intentions; whether they are conscious or subconscious. When you focus on something, you draw it to you. You must choose what you think about and focus your attention upon.

I know I can accomplish anything I focus upon!

This simple affirmation for some can be incredibly complex to assimilate and live, but has the ability to change your life.

Who do you want to be?

It is time to honestly appraise the following aspects of your life:

- Career
- Personal Development
- Money & Finances
- Self-Esteem
- Relationships
- Physical Health & Fitness
- Lifestyle or Quality of Life

Take the time to write 2-3 sentences on how you feel about the state of these aspects currently in your life.

Rate your satisfaction in each area on a scale of 1(needs drastic improvement) – 10 (perfect, no change needed, as good as it gets).

Satisfied is a tricky word. Can you ever have enough self-esteem or health? Much of life is subjective. This exercise helps to give you a perspective on what is working well in your life and what needs greater attention.

Many people will say "it is better than it was," others will say, "it is not as bad as some." That is not what you have been asked. Are you happy in each of these aspects of your life? This knowledge is imperative to not only improve the areas that need improvement, but especially to appreciate the areas in which you are doing well.

If you have great relationships, but do not appreciate them, they may fall apart as you focus your time on other areas. It is all about balance. Although some may need less time, it is crucial to give each area your attention.

If a person is a workaholic, their finances may be good, but their relationships may lack. If you are a fitness expert, you may focus more on the external body and ignore the inner personal growth. Each person has different strengths and weaknesses. One thing is certain, lack of balance leads to discord.

Balance takes consciously working in every area of your life. Some will require greater effort and attention than others. Every person has different areas of life that flow naturally and others may require some work. It does not mean anyone is better than another, just more balanced. Often, as a society, we see the outside effects and think somebody has it all together. Never compare your insides to another person's outsides. You never know what they truly think and feel. All people need to learn and grow. For some the areas in need are more apparent than others. Also, some are more willing to do the soul searching it takes to understand yourself and evolve. This is not a judgment, simply an observation. Some people would rather remain where they are than stretch into the uncomfortable feelings required to change.

Step #4

Joy is the only purpose of life.

To be truly content, or at least at peace with yourself, you must evolve each day. This means learning new things, being open to other's ideas and beliefs and allowing the next right thing to appear in your life. A flower does not go from a seed to full bloom in a day; neither will you. You must allow the seed a proper environment, give it light, water and allow nature to take its course. You must do the same. Allow for the unexpected, both good and bad. Learn how to adjust the sails as life changes course. Listen to your gut, your internal GPS, to trust there will be a next right thing presented. Some days that is easier than others, but it takes practice.

Many people were never taught the skills to adapt in life. You were often taught to plan, save money for that rainy day, listen to others and to be realistic. While none of these things are bad things, adventure, creativity, spontaneity and taking chances are also important in life. If you want different, you must be different. If you want more from life, you must allow it to express itself through you. The tangible is not all we have to believe in. It is the intangible that makes life exciting and wonderful.

Regardless of how you were taught, you get to choose how you live each day. You get to choose what you spend your time on. You get to choose what job, mate, friends and lifestyle you choose to live. Some people spend a lifetime living with the unconscious choices that others taught them to make. **It is time to wake up and claim your life.** It does not mean to go out and live recklessly, it simply means to realize that you can make the choices that bring you joy.

Living in joy means you light up from the inside. Joy and contentment radiates and cannot be hidden. A joyous person glows with bright eyes, a smile that is infectious and lives in exuberance for this day. If you have it, not only do you know it, but the world sees and feels it. It is an energetic presence in any room. It is a lightness brought to any problem. It is an inherent understanding that while you may not understand something now, you have the knowing that all is well! It is a peaceful understanding, a trusting that everything happens for a reason and that answers will be revealed in Divine timing.

That is a tall expectation for daily life. For most of us it starts with a glimpse of it. Then, possibly a day or a week of this bliss. But, trust that it can be a way of life. Know that if it is achievable by one human being, it can be achieved by any one of us. It has been seen in examples such as the Dali Lama, Mother Theresa, Jesus, Buddha and Mohamed. This does not mean they never knew times of fear, sadness or despair, it simply means they knew how to transmute every circumstance through love. This joyous existence is not just for the holy. It is exhibited by the teacher that takes special time with a student in need. Possibly by a nurse that calmed your nerves as you were being cared for. I witnessed this grace in an elderly aunt who, despite a very difficult life, exuded nothing but love. Perhaps you have a friend that when you speak with them, it feels as if in your time of need, nothing in the world seems to matter but you. This peaceful bliss is in the way any person can live their life, not by necessarily by extraordinary acts, but simple acts done extraordinarily with love. These examples exemplify self mastery, which occurs in most through practice. No person was born to live in despair. All are born to live in happiness, but sometimes you can fall in the pit of despair and not know you can climb out. Some people never knew they fell in and have spent years existing without hope. I assure you that you can live a beautiful life, but it takes releasing the fear, pain and resentment of the past. By reading this book, you are off to a good start or restart. Life does not need to be "fair" or "perfect" to be happy and fulfilled.

Step #5

Trust your internal GPS, your emotions.

Life is often filled with distractions. You may have set goals or establish priorities, but events happen and you were thrown off course. Often the best intentions can end up astray. So how do you know when you are off course? Your emotions are the internal gauge to help direct you to and through healthy changes in life.

It starts by determining the reason behind the goal or action. Everybody wants to have purpose in their life. The team with the greatest focus and passion wins any game. It is the same within any individual, company or group. You must know what you are working toward and for. The greater your personal purpose or passion, the greater your success will be at any task or in life. But it is important to remember that success is not about accumulating wealth, but living in joy.

Every person has a gut reaction, it is called instinct. When a car speeds down a street, instinct moves you away from that car. When the stove is hot, instinct prevents you from touching the pan or at least moves your hand away as soon as the sensation of heat hits. You can become just as in-tune to your emotions as well. You can trust your gut feeling to help keep you from negative circumstances.

You would never hire somebody you did not like; well you do not need to leave yourself in circumstances that diminish your feelings either. Staying at a job you hate is not healthy, yet we are often told the safe path is the right path. A good job is the one you feel good doing, not simply one that pays you.

There are times you must do things you would prefer not to, but you do not need to remain in undesired circumstances. If you are in any relationship, job or circumstance that does not feel right, trust your emotions, as it may be time for a change.

People may have told you how to act, what to say and how to live. Regardless of what you were taught, you get to decide how you choose to act and live now. There may be some choices that do not work out for you, but even the worst circumstances bring life lessons that determine your character; who you are and will become. Part of living consciously is asking yourself how you feel. Do not let others determine your path. If you are not used to asking yourself how you feel, it may take some getting used to. One basic rule to live by is to never accept unacceptable behavior from anybody, including yourself. Refuse to sell yourself short by living to make others happy.

Step #6

Move away from fear with each step.

There are only two core emotions: love and fear. Love is where we all want to be, but fear is what blocks it. I believe, as written in the book *A Course In Miracles*, "only love is real." To me fear is like when the clouds are blocking the sun; there may be darkness, but the sunlight still does exist. Regardless of your current circumstance, which may feel negative, the light is still within you. When somebody close to you dies, it is normal to feel grief, sadness and fear that you will never experience their presence again. While it may be true that you may never hold their hand or embrace them again; they are alive in every memory you possess of them. Every time you think of them, your love for them and memories of them, you give them life. It may be different from how you would choose it, but love never dies or goes away because it is real.

Fear is best expressed by the acronym **F**alse **E**vidence **A**ppearing **R**eal. I love this saying because it exposes fear for what it is, NOT REAL! It is the "what ifs, woulds, coulds and shoulds". It is never Truth, but only possible negative outcomes. It feels real. Sometimes it is debilitating. It can often keep you from change, growth and happiness. It is a natural innate response to life that you can learn to control.

Some basic fears:

- Not getting what I need or want. (food, clothing, shelter, control, job, mate)
- Other's opinion of me. (looks, status, job, control)
- My opinion of me. (how I truly feel… weak, insecure, not enough, guilt, shame)

- Losing what I have. (health, people, financial, control, respect)
- Disappointing God. (not enough, weak, unworthy)

Most people experience fear often. Fear is not terminally unique to you.

Remember, thoughts are things. As you think, so you attract to you. If you are afraid of what may happen, your focus, through the Law of Attraction, is attracting it to you. Monitor your thoughts and ask yourself "is this real?" Has it happened? Why am I wasting my time, energy and emotions on anything false? You can choose your thoughts, actions and beliefs, so choose consciously.

It has been proven that your thoughts are creative and manifest your life. Scientists have hooked electrodes up to a runner's brain and heart to monitor them while running a race and to others as they talked through a race. In both instances the results were the same. The brain treats the scenarios in your head the same as it does the ones you live through and physically experience. Both are just as traumatic to your body, mind and spirit. Why would you cause yourself physical harm by focusing on what you do not want?

Stress is the everyday acceptable term for of fear. Most people know they are stressed. But, what does that buzz word truly mean? Stress is a point of feeling overwhelmed by life; fear of not getting it all done, having too much to do, or not having enough time or resources. Again, it is not real, but certainly feels real. We all know there are physical results from stress such as: heart problems, digestive problems, loss of sleep, psoriasis, breathing problems, hair loss, anxiety, depression, ulcers, exhaustion, arthritis, memory disturbances, appetite loss, addictions and even outbursts of anger, just to mention a few. So with physical manifestations such as these, can you still question thoughts become things?

It is common to feel anxious in a new situation. The unknown can seem frightening, but without the new, greater joy could never be attained. If a child was not pushed out of their comfort zone, they would never attend the first day of school. If you never went on a first date, you could never fall in love. If you never started a new job, you could never advance. Discomfort is part of life when you grow. That is why they are called growing pains. While physical growing pains are in youth; growing pains occur emotionally in all stages of life.

The first step to mastering fear is to acknowledge when you have it. Fear is something I spent 30 years of my life ignoring, denying and avoiding. I pushed myself through life without acknowledging how I felt about it. I was taught to "handle" life. It was through that denial that I functioned for 15 years at nearly 400lbs. It allowed me to respond automatically; while the separation from my true self, kept me in crisis. I think of the word "handle" now and wonder what that even means.

Another inherent lesson learned in my youth was that strength meant doing it all by yourself; "it" being life. Today I realize how wrong that is. I realize it takes greater courage to admit what I do not know. It takes strength to ask for help. It takes faith to trust another by acknowledging my apparent "weaknesses." I am no better or worse than anyone else, just different, as we all are. It is those differences which bind us in our commonality and help us need each other in an important way. Needing each other is not the same as dependency. Every relationship and encounter should have some reciprocal value to you. Even giving to somebody in need helps you to feel needed.

Caring for the sick helps you to recognize your health. There are times you need to reevaluate. Are you giving and receiving enough in your life? If not, you may be blocking the vital Life Force to flow to and through you for your highest good.

Fear is not a weakness, but simply a blockage. So how do you release the blockage? Countless books have been written on stress and anxiety reduction. The best way to begin, as we did in this book, is by acknowledging how you feel now. What circumstance has you feeling this way? Is it real and can you do anything about it? Take care of yourself to the best of your ability. Do one thing at a time and stay in the light of Truth. Accept the truth about the circumstance, but do not be defeated by them. Most importantly, do the next right thing. In any situation, realize it is only temporary. This too shall pass. How you react in any situation is the choice that determines who you are. Life is not defined by what happened to you, but through you.

CHAPTER 3

Living in Balance

Is your life in balance?

Like a three legged stool, there are three aspects of life that must be
in balance to be happy.

- Physical (actual body)
- Spiritual (spirit-who you are, your personality traits)
- Emotional (thoughts, feelings, reactions)

If you are not in balance, you are left with a feeling of "there has to be
more to life than this." We have all thought this at times. The answer
to that question is always **YES, THERE IS SO MUCH MORE!!!!**

Physical

The body is the vessel with which we experience life. It can serve
to encourage or hinder your life experiences. Louise L. Hay has an
incredible explanation of disease as "dis-ease" in the body, a term
derived from _A Course In Miracles_. If there are manifestations of sickness in your life, you can learn a lot about healing the body by reading
her book _You Can Heal Your Life_.

Your body is the shell your essence or soul is presented to the world in. It is made up of two aspects: your medical and mental health as well as your physical attributes. It includes your health, age, race, gender, height, eye color, skin, hair, weight and every outer attribute including your clothing and style. It is also your self-esteem and how you carry and present yourself through that style, eye contact, posture and confidence. Some of these attributes you can control, while others you must come to terms with and accept or they will always block your joy.

Some physical attributes are hereditary. While you can easily alter your hair color and clothing; your height and race for example, were predetermined at birth. Confidence is determined mostly by the emotional aspect of self, it is displayed through the physical. As with many areas, they often overlap.

Personal body image is the major component to self-acceptance. I believe we are all part of a giant mosaic puzzle. No one piece is any more important than any other. We all have different, shapes, colors and sizes. You were created on purpose, with purpose to serve a purpose, which is what makes you beautiful and divine. As I stated earlier, the only way to live in peace is to make peace with your piece. Who you are and the role you play is how you exemplify your purpose. Your physical attributes are beautiful and help express who you are to the world. You must learn how accept and love yourselves enough to be comfortable and appreciate your piece of the Divine puzzle of life.

Spiritual

There is an Infinite Creator. A brain on a table does not think. A heart on its own does not beat. The same Infinite Creator that rises and sets the sun created you. I believe the soul within each person is a piece of that Divine Breath, which gives and releases life. People can help control circumstances such as some aspects of the environment, but do not determine which seeds will grow to harvest or on which days it will rain.

The spirit is who you are that makes you- YOU. It is the level of intensity or humor you bring to life through you. Your spirit is the part of you that loves and nurtures. Your spirit is the quirky aspect of you that make up your attitude and temperament. As an individual, that can be heavily influenced and changed by your environment. When your spirit is acknowledged and nurtured, it can be transformed into a tremendous source of strength.

Spirituality is the personal relationship between an individual with the Creator. Regardless of what you may or may not call this Source, we did not spontaneously come into this life. Purposeful connection of this through prayer, meditation, being in nature, faith, gratitude, service to another or any and all acts of love are some ways that we strengthen that connection.

Spirituality is often confused with religion. The Divine is not man-made. Religion, while considered Divinely inspired, is a particular path of beliefs and practices created by man. While religious practices can absolutely strengthen the spiritual connection, in some, they have also alienated many. Religion is not required to become a more spiritual person. There are many religious people that are not necessarily spiritual in their actions.

Spirituality is the most inner and personal aspect of the soul. There is no wrong way to connect, other than to disconnect. There are agnostics that believe it all happened by chance. I respect every persons individual choices and especially the birthright given for us to freely choose. I would be remiss if I did not boldly state that the life spent in this existence, in the true belief that chance is all there is, would be less than joy filled or fulfilled. To believe that the earth travels around the sun in perfect synchronicity is small minded. There is too much order in the tides, sunrise, genetics and science to prove it all could not happen by coincidence.

For the people that are reading this that I have just offended, I humbly ask you to act as if it were possible for something greater than man to exist. Entertain the possibility that the light and peace, love and joy you see in the eyes of a truly spiritual person are not coincidence. I have never seen a person without faith light up from the inside. I have never witnessed comfort in the factual interpretation of crisis. I ask you to witness a magnificent sunrise, the birth of a child, consolation of a dear friend or the transformation of a butterfly and honestly say there is nothing bigger than you at work in this world. Spirituality and emotions are intangible, but are very real! In fact they are what shape the reality that you live in.

Emotional

The driving force behind any action or reaction is your emotions. Thoughts are things, but emotion is what makes them manifest. When we focus upon a goal with optimism and confidence, it is assured. When we worry, it also attracts more to worry about. So why is it that we do not all have perfect lives?

Emotions are much deeper than the surface or conscious thought. They are the root of the matter; how you truly feel when all the distractions of life are removed. These are the things that keep you awake at night or the true reason behind procrastination and doubt. It is more than what you feel, but why you feel it. If you cry at a movie it is because of how you relate to it through your own past experiences. If you blunder your words at a job interview it is likely to be due to a lack of confidence more than poor preparation.

Often people or events in our life color our response to life. If you are the best at a particular sport, you tend to be more confident. If you have repeatedly fallen short of others or your own expectations, you may not have much confidence. The important part of this is that expectations are not fact, but ideas and perception. You are the only one that you need to impress. If you set your standards by others expectations, you will never fully control your own life, circumstances or happiness.

CHAPTER 4

Creating Your Breakthrough

Some pursue happiness, while others create it.

—unknown

Life is not about finding, but creating yourself. You must determine the type of person you want to be. You are only a product of your environment, if you allow it. You choose the environment you want to live in and the people with whom you surround yourself. Only you can determine your value and worth. You are limited by what you tell yourself or consistently allow others to tell you. Unfortunately, for some, that takes a lifetime to figure out.

The circumstances you were born into do not predetermine your worth, just your starting point. Your beginning is the point you start moving forward from in this lifetime. You are only limited until you make a different choice.

This was a harsh truth for me to own up to. It is easier to blame than to take responsibility. It is easier to settle, than to take action into the unknown. I came to realize that even after my college degree, I made the choices that kept me poor. It is easier to feel limited by circumstance than it is to take responsibility for it and change it.

Perhaps the most difficult lesson to really understand was the Law of Attraction. As much as I studied it, I did not understand the most important part to utilize it. To me it seemed to be common sense. Perfect examples were: a watched pot never boils, being destined for hereditary diseases, the adage that there is never enough money or whatever I do for that person is never enough. Perception is truth.

So why is your life not changing as you want it to?

If your thoughts become things, then what you focus on, with emotion, will come into your life. So I asked myself, why was it not working for me? I was a Life Coach that taught classes on goals and vision boards. Why was it not flowing into my life? Until one day I finally realized that subconsciously I was what was holding me back. As much as I tried to pretend I had the things I wanted, I still felt badly that I did not have them.

I finally understood that it was not about a lack, it was how I felt about the lack that kept me there. I believed poor was bad, so I was ashamed. I felt horrible that I was not financially successful, so I removed my personal power due to my negative, mostly subconscious emotions. No change occurred in my life until I realized that today is simply a starting point. Where you are is just the beginning, not good or bad. Recognize that only you determined your worth and only you can change it. It is not about luck or inheritance, but about empowerment.

Through the power of intention you are a powerful creator. Most wealthy people never fear poverty, which is why they stay wealthy.

Many poor people never get past their feelings of deprivation, which is why they continue to believe there is never enough. Most of this is not on the conscious level, but each individual creates and perpetuates it.

Fear, is the most powerful attractor because it consumes your emotions, which is where your power to create lies. The only way to break the cycle of attracting what you do not want is to be fully aware of your thoughts and emotions at all times. This may be a tall order, but it is possible over time. Every time you hear yourself saying or thinking thoughts that do not serve your purpose; let them go.

I chose to be poor, morbidly obese and taken advantage of for decades. Today I realize that I chose these things, certainly not consciously, through fear based thoughts and actions. I chose debt and struggle. I lived overwhelmed, which is what led me to quicksand of addiction, seeing no way out. Why would anybody choose that life?

My crisis continued until I realized it was not about simply denying where I was in life; I had to lovingly accept my circumstance and myself as I was without judgment in order for lasting change to occur. Why would anybody choose to spend almost 15 years of their life at 400lbs, in bankruptcy, in quiet desperation and in constant guilt? But, unconsciously, I did.

Today, I realize I held myself back due to my own insecurities. I admit this with great humility and understanding. I have earned character through difficulties and devastating pride leveling emotional and physical struggles. I offer this to you in hope that you will learn your lessons and have your awakening without that level of suffering.

I finally realized none of these events had the power to control my today or tomorrow. My victim and martyr mentality are what perpetuated the struggle and lack in my life. It was my guilt, shame, resentment and fear that kept me stagnant. As soon as I grasped that awareness, the gates of opportunity opened and I began attracting the positive things I had long desired and change flooded into my life. The moment I refused to be a victim and realized I was a creator, my power returned.

I may be the same individual, but I am changed inside. The story of the first 36 years of my life will not change, but from this point forward my life is anew, as a blank canvas. My experiences hold all the vibrant colors and pictures my heart desires.

- What old truths that no longer suit you have you been focusing on?
- What childhood habits or patterns do you need to break?
- What insecurities are you ashamed of?
- What are your fears?
- Where did they come from?
- What is the worst …or the best that could happen?

Step #7

Seek help if you get stuck or stumble.

On the first anniversary of my sister's death I was so consumed by trying to make other's feel better, that I did not give myself a chance to grieve. As a result, I was numb most of the day. It was easier to disconnect than to hurt. On the the 5th anniversary of her passing, I was still very emotional to the point of tears, but I acknowledged my own pain and got through it. I was aware that I miss her, but spoke about her and felt the grief and it passed like a cloud away from the sunlight of my spirit. I realize I cannot celebrate the gift she was to me with beautiful memories and be depressed at the same time. I can stay stuck in the pain or I can acknowledge it, allow it to hurt, but move through it. There are still times that a song comes on and I am instantly crying because I miss her physical presence, but then I allow it to pass without judgment and go on with my day. Sometimes that takes ten minutes and other days it takes hours, but it does pass. For a long time I would tell myself I "should" be used to this by now. That is ridiculous. Grief and sadness have no time table. Every person is different and is affected in different ways. I reiterate, pain will happen in life, but suffering is optional. When we ignore our true emotions or get stuck in the pain without seeking help, we are choosing to suffer. Pain will taint every day until we address it.

Sensitivity is not bad. You must honor how you truly feel. There will be times that people or situations disappoint you. It is up to each individual to release the anger, hurt, resentment and fear. Forgiveness, especially self-forgiveness, is a gift. In truth, all forgiveness is self-forgiveness. It is a release of negative emotion that allows the Light to shine through you again. It helps move away the dark ominous clouds of negative emotions that block your happiness. You may be right, but holding a grudge poisons only the holder. Would you prefer to be right or happy?

Journaling is an incredible tool to help get to the understanding of how you truly feel and why. Counseling can also help you get to the cause of unwanted patterns and emotions such as addiction, poor self-esteem, rage, despair, guilt, procrastination, lack of focus, chronic tardiness and lack of organization. All self-evaluation needs to be done lovingly and without judgment. When we can observe the action, without a reaction, we can often move into its awareness and no longer fall victim to it.

How do you know when you need help?

Many of us were raised to be "independent." That word can mean many different things, but is often taken as needing no outside help. It is often taught that to need help is a weakness. That is so far from the truth. As humans we need social interaction. It takes all different types of people that are good at all different things to have a full life. We are a social species. It is imperative to realize we all need help sometimes!

I love the statement that "it takes a village to raise a child." That statement is never finished by "and then the child grows up and moves out for a life of solitude." Although it can happen, that is not what this beautiful life was meant for. Love, the highest emotion there is, requires someone or something to love. Love is only fully appreciated when it is given and received. We are supposed to need each other!

When you do not know how to get to a better place, ask for help. Needing help is simply acknowledging that you are human. It is realizing that in this moment, life is not as you would choose it to be. It is a normal reaction to call a friend or loved one if you are upset. It is the same as a student asking a teacher or mentor for their experience, as simple as going to a mechanic when the car does not start or to a restaurant when we want a wonderful meal. It can seem difficult to ask for help. Some people are stubborn enough to lose years living in mediocrity rather than ask for help.

Knowledge can be taught, but wisdom comes through experience. Sometimes you must be wise enough to know what you do not know. There is no shame in not being perfect at everything. It is only when you feel the need to be perfect that life begins to feel pressured and overwhelming. For many, that is their natural state of getting through life, inherently trying to be perfect. Perfection is such a tall order. It is not possible in this plane of existence, at least not how most visualize perfection. In Truth, there is a reason or lesson in everything and there are less desirable outcomes, but no "wrong" choices.

You can never become perfect, because you were born that way. You were born with all the beauty and love of the Divine Creator within your soul in the moment you took your first breath. The more you try to be unlike your inherent perfection, the more misaligned you will feel. You cannot become great; you were already born with it. You were created on purpose for a purpose. Life is truly about allowing that greater meaning to unfold harmoniously in each new day as your life. Allowing that life to blossom into its perfection is natural and feels beautiful. Trying to change the color of the petals or the type of flower you were born to blossom into is uncomfortable and even painful. Emotional maturity is when you stop fighting and allow the greater good to flow through you out into the world. That will look as different to each as there are people on this planet. Just as each snowflake is different, but beautiful, so each individual is perfect by design.

CHAPTER 5

Emotional Maturity

Age has little to do with maturity. I have known children with greater sense of responsibility than some adults and some adults living life as a victim with all perceived wrongs happening to them. Age is simply a number, which marks another year in your body. That is all that it denotes. It is society and individuals that put expectations, both good and bad, on those numbers. Emotional maturity is the responsibility that develops within an individual. It comes with the understanding that every action creates a reaction and it is choosing more consciously for yourselves and those you love.

Five years ago I believed the common slogan: "that which does not kill you makes you stronger." After my sister's death, my mother's three cancer surgeries and as my father begins his latest treatment, after four prior cancer surgeries, custody battles, bankruptcy, two business closing and losing my home to foreclosure, which are just some of the things life brought me in a five years; today my view is different. I believe that although I am grateful for my faith and the strength that brought me through, I am very different than I was before these trials. Sometimes life has a way of thinning us out. Hardship can take a piece of you with it. Like a ship after a vicious storm; it may be afloat, but sometimes it is a bit worse for wear. I feel I lost much of youthful innocence and enthusiasm for life for a while due to grief.

Maturity is not just getting through an event or tragedy, but how it is handled. Getting through is automatic. Time will pass regardless of your choices. There will be storms and battles in life. How you handle them will determine how much of is left after the dust settles. Sometimes life is changed forever as when you lose somebody close. Often the greatest challenge and lessons are in the rebuilding of life after tragedy has swept through.

Some of the darkest battles are internal. Regret and guilt over the many would have, could have and should have's can destroy your connection with your soul if you allow it. The only true constant in life is change. Although you do have control over your life through the law of attraction, you cannot control the experiences of the people in your life. You can, however, learn to master your reaction to them. Being responsible means having awareness, acceptance and perseverance. Again, pain is inevitable, but suffering – remaining in that pain, is optional.

Maturity is taking responsibility in this moment to never be a victim again. It means consciously deciding in each moment to direct your sails toward your purpose. By spending too much time in the past, you rob the possibility of today. Come to trust that everything happens for a reason- though you do not always have to like that reason. The more you trust in the Great Divine, the less time you will spend suffering and the more you can appreciate today.

There are many things in your past and even present, that you would not have consciously chosen for yourself or for those you love to go through. You must accept what has happened and move through it to be able to appreciate the rest of the blessings in your life or it will continue to be a barrier to your joy today. In each moment the choice is always love or fear. When life is great love is easy. When life feels difficult, fear can seem to be an inescapable pit.

I realize I make that sound easy. Realize it is not a single choice, but making that same choice over and over again in each moment. It means controlling your thoughts, words and actions. It means having the maturity and strength to direct your sails, not fall victim to the storm, just for today. For many reading this it may bring up anger. How dare I make it sound so easy when life as they knew it is gone? You may have lost a job, your home, a loved one or even a child. It is not easy to pick up the pieces and move through, but the alternative is to just exist and not live. You get to make that choice.

A victim feels powerless over life. A victim is somebody who feels he or she is without free will or control over any possible change in life. A small child can be a victim, but it never needs to remain a victim. Adults may feel victimized, but in the free world, they get the choice to overcome any hardship and become a survivor. The human spirit is stronger than any problem or loss. But sometimes your inner connections are blocked. There are many people that feel betrayed by God. Some people choose anger to hide the sadness. It is easier to be mad than sad. That is why there are stages of grief. There is always help available to release the isolation and sadness and transform to vital and empowered individual. Sometimes it is a short distance that requires minimal outside help and other times it may seem like a desert with many resources needed. Maturity is not doing it all yourself, but realizing when you need help.

Emotional maturity is also when you use our inherent power to not just endure and get through life, but to thrive. Surviving is just existing, while thriving is living blissfully. Consciously you can call upon the life force within each breath to strengthen you. You can observe a situation without controlling or judging it. You can be still and ask its purpose; without needing to manipulate or deny it. You can learn from it without being weighed down by it. You can release it and heal without trying to force an outcome. Through the power of grace and faith, you can allow rather than resist or fight.

Power vs Force

Power is inherent in strength; fear is inborn of force.

Power is allowing Spirit to flow through you; force is pushing it away.

Power is the overflowing of abundance; force coerces the way.

Power is grace in bloom; while force is a crushing blow.

Power unfolds in perfection; force breaks down the door.

Power is a glorious embrace; force traps and holds without choice.

Power sees the internal rewards; force seeks bigger trophies.

Power's opulence is inherent; while force bullies respect.

Power glows and excites; force burns and destroys.

Power surges effortlessly; force pries between to separate.

Power grows eternally; while force is scarcity at its core.

Power is God's will in motion; force is want in action.

Power rests into life; force wrests from desire.

Power is a peaceful understanding; force thrusts its view upon the world.

God is powerful. Force is when I do not listen…again.

Step #8

Surround yourself with positive influences.

In your life there is your birth family and there are the people you will choose for yourself as your family. I was raised calling many people aunt or uncle who were not my blood relatives, but many of them I remain closer to them than my birth family. As human beings all of the differences we perceive are the result of one fraction of one percent of your DNA. Yes, we are greater than 99% the same; therefore we are all genetically "family." This is such an important fact to remember. We truly are all physically the same!

The term family changed for me so much as I got older. Family is so much more than blood relation. It can be described as the people who nurture and love you, not for what you do, but for whom you are. They are the people who know you best and appreciate you most. If you used that definition, are you spending enough time with family? Many people do not have enough people in their life that fill that role. If you feel that your current family is not giving to who you are, but simply depleting you, then the good news is you get a choice.

I am not telling you to abandon your roles in life; I am simply asking you to become aware of your roles. As a parent, child, friend, sibling, mate.... You get a choice in how you fulfill that role. You get choice in who you spend your time with and listen to. You get to consciously decide what your role is in each of your current relationships. If you feel they are unhealthy, determine how they got that way. In life, all are doing the best they can with the information they were given and decisions they have made. For many this is a stumbling block without realizing it.

Are you seeking the approval of others, for the appreciation you can only give yourself?

This may have been a lifelong pattern taught by the people you love. It was taught to them by the people they loved. In many cases it has been many generations of dysfunction that will continue until it is realized. You owe it to the people you love not to perpetuate dysfunction. The only way to do that is to examine each possible lie you have told yourself or each bit of negative self-talk you catch yourselves thinking and determine where it began; not with anger or blame, but to simply acknowledge it and dissolve it in the love of Truth.

Positive self-esteem requires truly knowing and living as your true self, regardless of the opinion of others. It allows you to rise up whether a challenge was thrust upon you or not. In this moment, you get to be the person you want to be, not who you were programmed or taught to be. That means regardless of how any other person treats you, you can be loving. You do not have to be guarded and distant or hurtful to people. You can consciously choose to always be loving. But, no longer allow them to be hurtful to you. That is called boundaries. There are very few "have to's" in this life. Today I challenge you to determine the difference between the people you have to spend time with and the people you choose to spend time with. If a family member is toxic to your well-being, lovingly release them. If you feel, not others tell you, that you must care for them, than find a way to do it without depleting yourself in the process. If an elderly parent is verbally abusive, help pay for their care. If an adult child is hurtful, let them know in a loving way. You help determine your worth by how you allow others to treat you.

Codependency is very common in relationships, especially if you were raised to be a care-taker. I was raised to make others happy. I was inherently taught that my happiness was to be found in giving joy to others. While that proved true in many cases, it spent decades depleting me and eventually led me to a food addiction I used to fill the void of love I gave to everyone but myself. There are many books to be found on healthy relationships. Wonderfully insightful authors and relationship experts like Iyanla Vanzant and Melody Beattie can help.

How could you understand and practice healthy boundaries and relationships if you were never taught them?

You can learn about healthy relationships now. If a relationship causes you pain it may be an unhealthy relationship to be looked at. Not every person you meet is meant to be center stage in your life for the entire show. You get to choose with whom you continue to share your life. You may need to move out of your comfort zone. You may need to go new places to meet people with similar interests. Life is meant to be uncomfortable at times, which can be the excitement that leads to positive change.

I am warning you to expect some disapproval from the people that liked you taking care of them. Try to understand it was not all their doing. You allowed the relationship to be formed this way. They have expectations based on how it was and now you are different, but they are not. It is not about right or wrong. You deserve to live in reciprocal relationships, but that was not what you helped create. This is to encourage you to understand their point of view as well. The new, healthier and happier you will not always get met with resounding approval. But, it is imperative for your lasting peace of mind to establish healthy relationships and a healthy support system.

Your support system is the people you can count on in a time of trouble or sorrow, not just when you life appears to be going well. These are people that will be honest with you and have your best interest at heart. The true loved ones that know you, often even better than you know yourself. It is a blessing to have somebody that can be brutally honest with you for the highest good and in a loving way. But it takes maturity to be able to hear constructive criticism and appreciate it. It takes strength to assimilate it without guilt, shame or self-doubt; to be able to use it to become even stronger. If you do not feel you have a support system in place, it is time to create one. Some people are born into it, but others must cultivate one for themselves.

Unfortunately, children are not born with instruction manuals. Your parents were not given tangible lessons or taught how to allow your colors to shine. They were taught by their parents, who were taught by theirs and they all did the best they could, as we all do. But if you are reading this now, you know the Truth. It is not true because I say it. It is Truth, when it calls out to your soul and initiates a response of "yes." When it already lives and breathes within you in total honesty and perfect love, which is Truth. "Be still and know" in the silence is often how you will hear or come to understand the Truth. There is an inner knowing, not as you may have been taught, but by how you feel. Trust the still small voice within you only when it is loving and nurturing, not when it echoes the sentiments of people who spoke from their own pain and may have contributed to your pain. Only believe the Divine Mother, Father, God, Creator of all that gave you breath and purpose. If you feel disconnected from that Divine Love, begin by being still and quiet. Then, read or listen to many different spiritual teachers or preachers. Seek inside and outside for something that stirs your soul, not just your intellect. Spirituality is meant to be felt, experienced and lived; not necessarily as you were taught by your human parents, but by your Divine Parent and Creator. You may, at times, need help realigning with that connection. On a soul level, you will know the Truth when you feel it. If you have not felt it yet, keep searching. It is absolutely worth the peace and fulfillment it brings.

This spiritual alignment with Truth is by far the most important aspect of true lasting happiness. Unfortunately, it is often the least explored. Remember anything outside of us is temporary, but the soul is eternal. The people, events and circumstances in life are forever changing, but who you truly are, your purpose, never does. Spend some time asking yourself some deeper questions about life. If you do not know the answers as they would pertain to you, for you, in your life, please give yourself the gift of traveling past the tangible and journey into the timeless aspect of Truth.

- What do I believe in?
- What is most important to me?
- Who or what created all I can see or know?
- What is my connection to that Creator?
- Does it or could it help me in my daily life?
- What is my life purpose?
- How could I strengthen that connection, to find or live my purpose?

These are some very deep philosophical questions for which there is no wrong answer. The important part is to know, not as others taught you, but for yourself. What is your truth? Many people never ask, yet look around at their external life and ask "is this all there is?" The answer is always NO!!! But you must remember that nothing external can ever fill an internal void! There is so much more than what you can see, but you must search for it. You must discover the answers for yourselves. For some it will be studying and meditating, while for others it may take a Spiritual Coach, member of clergy or preacher, books or even a spiritual retreat to help know or remember what you truly believe and why you believe it. As emotional maturity develops, seeking naturally transforms to understanding and guiding others.

I cannot stress the importance of spirituality enough on your path for a fulfilled life of bliss. To go through life strictly intellectually is like watching a 3D movie without the glasses. You are a sentient being that feels so much more than you see. You must consciously live from the inside out or you will not have any control of your direction and joy in life. Your spirit is who you were meant to be. To squash that spirit is like telling a child they can only watch others on the rides at an amusement park, but cannot get on any of the rides themselves.

Are you living life as a bystander or actively participating?

Realize that you get choice in each moment. You can choose your work, your companions and your surroundings. When you fully realize this, each moment may not seem joyous, but your life will be. You will be fulfilled because even in sad moments, your heart and soul know your way back Home.

CHAPTER 6

Creating the Life YOU Want!

On _Your Journey to Happiness_, it is imperative to figure out what YOU really want. The sooner you figure this out, the quicker you are enjoying life. What are your dreams and goals? What do YOU want? Many people just get by. They do what is expected of them next and wonder why they do not feel fulfilled. Many people do not even know what makes their heart sing or what makes them excited.

It begins by discarding others' plans for your life and asking what do you really want? Many people are living in somebody else's box. It is time to break out of the constraints of your life and dream.

If you could step out of your life and into the life of your design, what would be different?

Some things to go by are:

1. It is often not what others expect of you.

2. It may not be what you expect of you.

3. It is often not simply defined or may be anything you have ever been exposed to.

4. There is no wrong answer.

5. It will often change as you grow and evolve.

6. If you realize a change, be still for a while and ask yourself why it has changed. Be certain it is for the right reasons.

Some possible deterrents to positive change:

a. Not "realistic"

b. Too difficult

c. Not acceptable to others

d. Past patterns

e. Feeling unworthy

f. Lack of anything-time, resources, intelligence, motivation, focus

Be certain to be authentic and honest. This is not what most are taught, but it is the only way to live and remain in joy. If you are in the vocation that you were born for, it does not feel like work. It is always rewarding, but in different way. I consider a stay at home mom as one of the most difficult vocations, the position receives no salary, but is certainly a noble calling. Many artists struggle, at least for a while, but their passion fuels their soul. Remember that money is only one means of compensation.

Joy is not external. There is no external thing that can fill the internal void of passion. That excitement is not always fueled by our vocation. These are some areas of your life to look at if you are feeling depleted, disconnected or bored:

- Relationships (family, romantic, friendships)
- Hobbies

- Religious affiliations or connection
- Occupation
- Charities you contribute resources to (time or money)

In what aspects of your life are you not feeling fulfilled?

It may be one or all. It may also be the eyes you are looking through. If you happened to miss that line, I will repeat it. **Is there something wrong or simply how it is perceived by you or others?** If you do not take the time to truly discern how you feel, you cannot make it better.

Now that is a deep question I have pondered many times. After years of "working on me" in counseling, 12-step work, books, classes, lectures, meditation, one of the greatest truths I realized was that I did not feel worthy; therefore, I did not trust myself and often sabotaged my own efforts. Even as I write this my ego's insecurities (which we all have) are raging at me. My ego is telling me to never say it out loud or especially write it down. When you acknowledge the dark stuff inside, the Light shines upon it and it no longer rules you. It may peek through occasionally, but it no longer weighs you down physically or emotionally. For me, I ate over my emotions. The excess or unhealthy foods "punished" and numbed me so I did not feel. It was how I "escaped" and the cause of decades of pain in addiction. The more I recognize the Light, the less I lean toward the darkness. For me, it took me realizing both intellectually and subconsciously that who I am has little to do with what I look like and everything to do with how I treat others and myself.

All people are works in progress. Just as a painting is not complete until the last brush stroke, you too are not finished until your last breath. A beautiful lesson to master is that regardless of your perception, you are complete right now. The only thing you must truly do is to realize it. While you consistently get to add another page every day of your life, know that you are enough right now. If this was your last page, you would never be upset because you did not own the right car or house. It would not be about finishing a degree or taking one more vacation. The greatest realization you can have is to appreciate who you are right now. Acknowledge the loving relationships that live through you. Marvel at all of your blessings right now and not deplete one more moment on what is not. Accept the truth, that in this moment you have, you do and are enough! Please take a moment and appreciate your path which took you to where you are so that you can honestly discern what you will plan next. You can see the cup as half full or half empty, but either way you have no reason to thirst. Appreciate what is in your life or you have nothing to build upon.

Step #9

Never lose focus of your dreams.

Your dreams are the blueprints for your life that you draw up. They are the goals and action steps that make up the steps to the external and internal life you want. Hundreds of books have been dedicated to goal setting. Please do not be the perfectionist that I wanted to be, do not buy a dozen books on the subject to try to figure out the perfect way to do something. Just as I learned about meditation, exercise and many other things in life, the only wrong way to set goals is to not start. Yes, by researching and planning, I will not make a mistake...but that is the mistake. Life is supposed to be experimental not researched. Yes, we can learn from other's mistakes, but some things we must learn for ourselves. Your path is unlike any other. There is nobody on this planet exactly like you. There never was and never will be. You are the perfect YOU! You are perfect at it now. As you live and learn you expand intellectually, spiritually and experientially, but you are a perfect expression of the Divine's creation right now!

Please take some time with that thought. Go to a beautiful place in nature, physically if you can or even in your mind. See the beauty which surrounds you and realize you were designed perfectly by the same Creator. You are as beautiful to the Sculptor as the ocean, sunset or even a rainbow. You were designed and born of the same miracle worker that they were. It is up to you to decide to live in that recognition. That is not in arrogance, but appreciation of the Artist.

The most important aspects to goal setting is writing them out and reviewing them regularly. It changes it from a wish to a plan. It will change the completion rate of achieving the goal by over 90%. You make lists for the grocery store, but do you do it for your life? Do you research which computer to buy, but apply to work at any company that will take you? You may plan a vacation months in advance and often save money for it even longer, but do you invest in classes, a retreat or a Life Coach to help you succeed in the life of your dreams?

Realize from this moment forward that you are not a victim of your past unless you perpetuate it. Whatever path brought you to this moment was the right one for you. It made you who you are, which led you to this book. The purpose of this book is to help you realize that you are the designer of your life. Your thoughts from the past brought you to this moment, but your thoughts right now are just as creative and will deliver your future. What are you thinking, planning or deciding? If you are not doing it consciously, be careful, because you are doing it every moment of every day. Thoughts are things and so are your dreams as soon and as often you dare to dream, plan and step toward them. The only things you can never achieve are the things you never try. As Gandhi said, "be the change you wish to see in the world." **Be the hero of your life story!** Each powerful wave in the ocean began with a rain drop. Every mighty oak tree was once a small acorn. You are as mighty and powerful as anything in nature because of the Force that gave you your first breath and the one you take as you now read this. The only thing ever holding you back is you. Dare to dream and plan accordingly. **Regardless of your past, you can determine your happy ending.**

Just as important as claiming your goals, you must make them in every area of life. The most successful or wealthiest people are not necessarily the happiest. To be fulfilled and live in joy, you must see it as more than a destination spot as on a vacation, but the manner in which you live. You must balance the three aspects of self: physical, spiritual and emotional. All of your goals should not be tangible.

What good is the beautiful home without a wonderful marriage of the people who live inside? While relationships may not be a destination, you can work toward and see notable improvement. You do not need a mate to be happy in life. The healthiest you- physically, emotionally and spiritually, will attract and perpetuate the healthiest relationships.

Step #10

Be open to even greater dreams.

To be and remain happy you must appreciate yourself as you are every step along your journey. It requires living in integrity and treating others as you want to be treated. There is a law of Karma; what comes around goes around. Be conscious of the manner in which you live or you may again be the one holding yourself back.

Realize your view and point of view will change with you and be open to the beauty and love that comes with each lesson, challenge and perceived problem. Remember that "this too shall pass." Growing pains hurt and they can happen at any age. Because, the only thing you are ever truly becoming is more aware.

Allow Life to lead you as much as you lead it. Yes, maintain control of your ship, but also listen to the still small voice in you that is ready to explore. Just as you see infinite possibilities in your children from birth, know the Divine Creator also sees that potential in you. Just as a child takes its first steps and eventually begins to walk, then run; you too will do the same as you see your dreams come to fruition. You will never know what you can achieve until you try and once you get a taste of that fulfillment and the grace it brings, joyful expectation will be your garment of choice. Be open to even greater blessings than you can even conceive; the more you have, the more you have to offer others and remember that blessings are not only physical.

Trust yourself enough to begin. Love yourself enough to continue and appreciate yourself enough to recognize your success. The greatest measure of success is not your bank account, but your spirit. The simplest task done with love can be a kindness that is never forgotten.

The blanket my "Aunt" Angie made me as a child is one of the most beautiful gifts I ever received and she thought so little of it, she left it on my front steps. But, knowing she made those blankets with such love only for her grandchildren is why I keep and appreciate it so much today. It is not what you do or give, but the manner in which you live that will fill and fulfill you. As you help fill others, trust the Universe to fill yours in greater ways than you could ever imagine.

Whether the cup is half full or half empty and regardless of the style or size of the cup, never be afraid to drink from it and be grateful that you are not thirsty. Appreciate what you have now and it will continue to grow; but the fear that it is not enough will certainly lead you on the fear-full path of "never enough." You can choose your focus, direction and pace on your path, but please never lose sight that it is all choice and at any moment you get to adjust your sails.

CHAPTER 7

Tool Kit

To help and keep YOU happy.

This chapter briefly examines fifteen of the greatest intangible tools you can use to joyously navigate on your path. The beauty of these assets is that they are all free and accessible at any time or circumstance. There are countless books written on each. I encourage you to utilize them to their fullest. The more you recognize and develop these tools in your daily life, the greater your happiness will be. This chapter is a perfect place to restart your path when you feel off. By reading the list, which is in no order of importance, your inner voice will guide you to the one you need most in any moment.

15 Tools of Joy

Hope	Laughter	Faith
Grace	Passion	Peace
Love	Forgiveness	Gratitude
Balance	Patience	Awareness
Health	Spirituality	Serenity

Life is not a riddle with a definite answer. It is all an exploration of circumstances and opportunities. All begin and end in very different places. The beauty is in realizing you can guide the sails to take you where you want to be and with whom you choose to share it with. You need not be a victim to circumstance any longer; you are the author of your life.

If you are reading this book, you have the ability to change your life completely by simply changing your perspective. You choose your view. By shifting your perspective on any of the fifteen tools in this chapter, you will shift your mood, your day and your life. Your view is your truth.

What are you focusing on, your blessings or your problems?

Do you see choice or other's expectations?

Do you want to take control of this moment or blame others for the current view?

It is not easy to look inside at the cause of your sadness, hurt or grief. It is much easier to blame or deny it, but the more aware you are of your own emotions and patterns, the less you will veer off your path of joy. You will not be in the state of bliss in every moment, but it will grow as you practice self-honesty and self-love. The work you have done on yourself by answering the questions in this book are a tremendous gift to yourself. You are worth the effort and you deserve to be happy.

There is a daily journal I wrote which is available to accompany you on your path of awareness called _Your Journal to Happiness_. The book is a complementary tool which takes only five minutes per day to help you maintain the deep level of honesty and awareness you have taken on your journey through this book. It will help keep you focused and in gratitude; which will enhance each life experience.

Hope

Hope is defined as:

: to desire with expectation of obtainment

: to expect with confidence : <u>trust</u>

Hope is the wonder of all beauty and blessings to come. It is the magnificent unknown, when we accept and allow the Divine to perfectly unfold each day. It is the heart believing in the highest outcome. It is trusting God to be God and not trying to figure out how it will all work. With the innocence of a child, it is expecting and knowing that all is well. It is the optimistic view of the soul. It is why we teach our children about fairy tales and Santa Claus. It is the joyful desire which awaits our beckoning as much as we await its promise.

There are many people who are thinkers and planners and want to figure it all out. They only believe in what they can see and do themselves. Some were taught this by parents, while others learned it through disappointments. There will be displeasure in life, but it need not be your fate, only a moment to make the next success even brighter.

Hope is trusting for the highest possible outcome, not because it is logical, but simply as the motivation which guides us through life joyfully. Life is not on your personal time table, but is Divinely timed. By allowing it to unfold perfectly, you do not rush through and miss today. It is not sitting still and waiting for Life to deliver our wish list, but listening and paying attention to your guided path. It is helping you take the next right step.

As it is on any trip where the destination is desired, life is exciting. Hope helps you eagerly anticipate each new day and opportunity. It allows for the bumps and even detours in the road without dimming the enthusiasm for your desired outcome.

Hope is a wellspring within your heart. It is why people pray. It is why and how you believe in what you cannot see. It is trusting your intuition for your highest good. It is an emotional offering for the joy to come.

Some examples of things big and small you may hope for: world peace, promotion, health, wealth, weather, family bonds, gifts, cures of disease, parking spots and even sporting event outcomes. There are so many areas in life you can practice hope. But, when you practice hope, it must be with positive emotions as a prayer for good and it should feel good. It is giving in positive awareness and expectation. Thoughts are things and the good intensions will certainly be returned to you, although not always when or how you may expect it.

Grace

Grace is defined as:

1) *a* : unmerited divine assistance given humans for their regeneration or sanctification; *b* : a virtue coming from God; *c* : a state of sanctification enjoyed through divine grace

2) *a* : <u>approval</u>, <u>favor</u>; *b: archaic* : <u>mercy</u>, <u>pardon</u>; *c* : a special favor : <u>privilege</u>; *d* : disposition to or an act or instance of kindness, courtesy, or clemency; *e* : a temporary exemption : <u>reprieve</u>

3) *a* : a charming or attractive trait or characteristic; *b* : a pleasing appearance or effect : <u>charm</u>

Grace is an intangible comfort of the soul available to all. It has nothing to do with religion and is not earned or acquired. It can only be allowed through your awareness. It is a feeling of lightness, power and strength given by the Divine. It is yours in the moments you allow ourselves to be more than do. It is an allowing of energy that lifts you emotionally and physically to better than you naturally were or would be in a particular moment or circumstance.

Grace is often disguised as coincidence, which is God's way of remaining anonymous. It may be that second wind when you desperately need to meet a deadline. It is the light that shines from within in a time of sorrow or the call from the perfect person in just the right moment. It is a feeling of protection and lightheartedness. She is Lady Luck and the angelic right answer that comes through as your thought or intuition to solve a problem or a new invention to meet your needs. It is a feeling of favor and encouragement provided by an internal or external source in ways you could never plan for or conceive of.

The greatest ways to cultivate grace are the spiritual practices of prayer and meditation. There are no magical or universal specific rules to prayer. Prayer is simply talking to the Creator and meditation is listening. The best way to pray is for the highest and best of all concerned, not just your desired outcome. As you practice listening, grace cannot help but fill you with its understanding. Every mystic that ever lived received answers in the silence. The difference is they were listening, understood and trusted.

One of the greatest gifts you can bestow on your fellow man is your graceful presence. That is a state of being present to them and for them in loving service. This beautiful blessing you bestow any time you listen or help without expectation, judgment or direction. It is being, not doing; allowing, not directing. This is every soul's purpose in some way, but requires leaving the ego aside and allowing the Love you were created with and for to shine through you. In those moments it is clear we are the messengers and in the presence of Divine on earth.

Love

Love is defined as:

1) *a (1)* : strong affection for another arising out of kinship or personal ties <maternal *love* for a child> *(2)* : attraction based on sexual desire : affection and tenderness felt by <u>lovers</u> *(3)* : affection based on admiration, <u>benevolence</u>, or common interests, *b* : an assurance of affection <give her my *love*>

2): warm <u>attachment</u>, enthusiasm, or devotion

3) *a* : the object of attachment, devotion, or admiration; *b (1)*: a beloved person : <u>darling</u> —often used as a term of endearment *(2) British* —used as an informal term of address

4) *a* : unselfish loyal and benevolent concern for the good of another: as *(1)* : the fatherly concern of God for humankind *(2)* : brotherly concern for others; *b* : a person's adoration of God

5) : a god or <u>personification</u> of love

6) : an <u>amorous</u> episode : <u>love affair</u>

7) : the sexual embrace : <u>copulation</u>

8) : *capitalized Christian Science (and several other religions)* : <u>god</u>

Love is so much more than a feeling; but certainly the highest emotion there is. It is so much more than a description, for it is truly what gives life purpose. It is the expression of Divine in, as and through us. The only true factor is how much you recognize it; in people, nature and life.

Unconditional love has no expectations and can never be done imperfectly. It is an intangible giving that has the power to heal sadness, pain and even the eternal sense of separation. It is a blessing best given unintentionally. It is the natural state all are born into and the best way to live. It is a piece of your essence given and a piece of another's essence received. Love is truly all there is; the rest of life is simply a distraction.

There are several kinds of love: self-love, family, friends, romantic, hobbies, of nature and Divine. It is pure pleasure and the highest vibration you can offer. To be in a loving place is coming home, because the truest home is your soul and love is all it knows and can recognize. Any time you feel cut off from this bliss; remember it is always inside of you. It is what makes up the spark of Divine inside you which allows in every breath. It is always present, but sometimes you may feel isolated and blocked from it. Just as there is never truly darkness at night, just the rotation of the planet away from the sun or as in any dark room, you can flip the switch to illuminate the Truth. Love is always present and the more often you show it to others; through kindness, concern and presence, the more it will be revealed for you. You cannot be a channel of love without receiving its blessings. It is equally beautiful to give and receive and is what makes life worth living.

Love can be cultivated through random acts of kindness, beautiful memories-especially of children, forgiveness and appreciation of nature, nurture and Life itself.

The symbol of love is the heart, which is the strongest muscle. As with any muscle, you can develop it with use. It is the central life force of the body and love is the life force of the soul.

Balance

Balance is defined as:

1) : a counterbalancing weight, force, or influence

2) *a* : stability produced by even distribution of weight on each side of the vertical axis

b : equipoise between contrasting, opposing, or interacting elements

c : equality between the totals of the two sides of an account

3) *a* : an aesthetically pleasing integration of elements

b : the juxtaposition in writing of syntactically parallel constructions containing similar or contrasting ideas

4) : mental and emotional steadiness

More details of the aspects of balance are in Chapter 3; the three aspects of physical, emotional and spiritual. It takes focusing upon and developing all areas of life to maintain happiness. Any time you catch yourself saying "if I had_____, I would be happy," remember life is not a destination, but a process of managing all aspects of life. While physical and financial goals are a great way to focus and accomplish some things in life, they will never produce long term joy.

Balance imperative to fulfill, not just fill any perceived void in life. Most of the time when you experience an ache of something missing, it is an internal hole that can only be filled by non-material things. It may be your artistic side longing to get out or perhaps your inner child in need of some fun through hobbies or exercise. Your emotions are the greatest measure of life's balancing act. If you are not in alignment, it leaves a feeling of "is this all there is." That is when you must review your schedule, relationships and daily life and determine what aspect may be in need of attention.

Life wants to be in balance and will often bring needed change that can help even the keel. It is up to you to adapt, recognize the lesson in any circumstance and allow it to flow in Divine timing. Many people feel they spend their life swimming upstream. If you are feeling that way, you are pushing against Life. Just for this day, allow the tide to carry you forward. Trust the waves of Universal Law and Truth, to provide for you in every way. Allow the Creator to create. Miracles cannot occur when you do not trust and accept them. Life cannot provide for you what you struggle to provide or accept for yourself.

Health

Health is defined as:

1) *a* : the condition of being sound in body, mind, or spirit; *especially*: freedom from physical disease or pain; *b* : the general condition of the body

2) *a* : flourishing condition : well-being ; *b* : general condition or state

Perfect health is a state of wholeness, mentally and physically. It is being free of all illness or discontent. It is your natural state and what your soul or gut will always guide you toward when you pay attention. It is a place of harmony where all aspects of life are working together perfectly. Your cells know inherently to regenerate and heal without your direction. It is the natural state for the body and mind and all of nature.

Resistance and discord are the greatest disturbance to health. There are some things in life you must allow that you may not appear to want. This feeling can cause stress on the body and mind. Stress is a state of feeling pulled or overwhelmed by circumstances physical and or emotional. Usually there are external triggers. Disease is a state of "dis- ease" in the body. Negative emotions manifest as physical conditions. Louise Hay offers an index of the internal beliefs that manifest as particular illnesses in her book <u>You Can Heal Your Life</u>, it has even been turned into even an incredible phone application. Its accuracy on the correlation of internal circumstances as the cause of external diseases is beyond coincidence. This knowledge is not to place blame, but to allow the awareness of it to change the belief that caused the disconnection from Source and restore wellness.

Perfect health takes balance in all aspects of life, as explained in Chapter 3. It requires paying attention to the physical, emotional and spiritual aspects and needs in your life. It is not simply external. Happiness is completely internal; yet it is external conditions which often restrict or allow and maintain joy. You do not need perfect health to experience a fulfilling life, but it does help.

Some illnesses are considered hereditary, which predisposes a person due to their family's history. There are those that believe simply the belief in that can attract it to you. Regardless of how an illness manifests, many can be treated, but not cured medically. Many can be improved upon by a better mental attitude and positive expectations. Your positive attitude is imperative to lasting good health. Regardless of any apparent dis-ease, as with any outer circumstance, it does not need to determine or limit your happiness. Although poor health is often a distraction, joy is not derived from any external or physical circumstance.

Mental health is the most important aspect of all. When this is off, life can feel impossible to improve. There are times chemical imbalances can throw off the mental equilibrium and it is as if you were wearing an unfocused set of glasses that you cannot take off and many do not even know the picture is skewed. Sometimes it is a result of something as simple as less melatonin from less sunlight in the winter time, some suffer in addiction, while others are chemical misfires in the brain such as ADD, bipolar disorder or even clinical depression. There are many reasons for mental misalignment or distorted thinking and behavior. The medical community has thankfully made tremendous strides in its ability to diagnose and treat a wide variety of illnesses. It is up to the individual or parent of a minor, to advocate for the best care. In many circumstances medications can help bring the mind and body into alignment. It is important to understand that if any person is compromised mentally in any way, it is not a choice. Nobody would choose the pain of not being able to adjust to or deal with life. Support them and treat them lovingly, especially if it is you. Everyone is born with different traits or physical conditions, not chosen, but predetermined, but they need not be considered afflictions and many are treatable. For some it is a result of trauma or tragedy. Be compassionate and patient and know that all deserve and can have the highest and best in this lifetime. Everyone has work to do in self understanding, for some this is their greatest challenge. Be certain to remain in alignment with all aspects of life to be certain to receive the greatest benefits of care and achieve and remain in your best health.

Laughter

Laugh is defined as:

1) *a* : to show emotion (as mirth, joy, or scorn) with a chuckle or explosive vocal sound ; *b* : to find amusement or pleasure in something; *c* : to become amused or derisive

2) *a* : to produce the sound or appearance of laughter; *b* : to be of a kind that inspires joy

Laughter is a physical action and a release of joy. It is an instant transformative healing energy, which lifts your outlook and mood instantly. It is the quickest way out of fear or despair. It is contagious and will spread happiness to all around you. When you laugh, it sends a physical message of energy and joy to every cell in your body.

It does not matter if it is by hearing a joke, watching a comedy on tv or going to a comedy club. It is an act of seeing or acknowledging with a lightness of spirit. It is a release of apparent problems or concerns and an allowing of contentment. Since what you focus upon is attracted to you, it is a great practice to attract better feelings and circumstances in life.

Tomorrow's possible problems and responsibility too often weigh on you and can rob today's blessings. Laughter helps you to not take life too seriously. Children laugh and play as their purpose, until adults thrust their own fears upon them. They are taught to not act carelessly, but sometimes those carefree moments are exactly what are needed. Remember, you get to choose your life- your job, friends, hobbies and how you spend each moment of your day. Be certain you are choosing consciously, not out of habit or the influence of others.

The purpose of this book is YOUR happiness, so take this tool as a daily practice. The soul, body and mind want to feel good. Laughter is an instant way to experience acute joy. So spend more time with young children and allow them to teach you how to have fun. I often recognize myself taking circumstances too seriously. It helps me to spend a few minutes blowing bubbles, especially at the ocean. For less than a dollar, it is simple stress relief in a bottle with no side effects. I keep bubbles at the office and in the car and do not care what people think. It is freeing to release my inner critic and laugh at myself.

Be silly. Be free. Be happy!!!

Passion

Passion is defined as:

1) the state or capacity of being acted on by external agents or forces

2) *a (1)* : emotion *(2) plural* : the emotions as distinguished from reason; *b* : intense, driving, or overmastering feeling or conviction; *c* : an outbreak of anger

3) *a* : ardent affection : love; *b* : a strong liking or desire for or devotion to some activity, object, or concept; *c* : an object of desire or deep interest

Passion is an internal fire that excites and motivates your thoughts, words and actions. It is a purpose that empowers you to grow in focus. It is the use of talents or inspiration to guide and nurture your soul and life. It excites you with an intangible push for action.

An activist believes in their cause, such as: feeding the poor, peace, human or animal rights or even curing a particular illness, at a soul level .They are called to devote their resources- time, talents, money or prayers. It is a particular focus that they feel enriches their life and that of others. Many believe it is a purpose they were born to fulfill. The rewards service offers is so much greater than financial.

Often, when a person feels frustrated or discontent with their job, it is a time for a life review. The reason for life is joy and love. If how you spend your time does not encourage growth and empowerment, it will leave a void. Life is meant to change and each soul has an altruistic desire to serve a higher purpose. It is not always fulfilled through vocation; it is often a hobby or interest. Regardless of how it is explored or experienced it is powered through faith and inner guidance. Trust your instincts and talents enough to share your calling. It will add a dimension to life that nothing else can fill.

Forgiveness

Forgive is defined as:

1) *a*: to give up resentment of or claim to requital for; *b* : to grant relief from payment of

2) to cease to feel resentment against (an offender) : <u>pardon</u>

Forgiveness is the greatest gift you can ever give yourself and all forgiveness is self forgiveness. It is a release of pain and hurt that completely blocks the light of joy. The greater the hurt you hold, the dimmer life will appear. It will also keep you from trusting others or Divine.

Forgiveness does not sanction what anyone may have done to you as acceptable behavior. It is your emotional acceptance that it happened. The realization that it is time to release the pain that it holds within you is crucial for your happiness in life. You do not need to speak with the person you forgive, but you must let go of all the bitterness or thoughts of revenge. The poisonous thoughts will continue to keep you from your joy. If you look at the definition, it has nothing to do with the receiver, the venom only effects the holder or person that needs to forgive.

My minister and teacher, Reverend Ian Taylor, best explained forgiveness by completely wiping a blackboard clean. There were no remnants left behind to determine what was there before. The slate was completely empty. True forgiveness means to forgive and forget and never return to the thoughts and emotions again. It is a complete release of past blame, shame or burdens. That clear example helped me to see how often I thought I had forgiven, but had not forgotten, so the wound in me was not healed.

For me, self forgiveness was and remains the most difficult. I have always been hardest on myself. I spent 15 years at almost 400lbs and many more between 250-350lbs. My food addiction kept me in layers of guilt, shame and fat. I knew how to eat properly and could even help others to lose weight, but my guilt and self-mutilating habits kept me subconsciously punishing myself. I have done much work to forgive myself and release the layers of hurt. Consciously, I know I was a scared and lonely child that used food to get through life. Consciously I forgave myself completely, yet the thoughts and patterns persisted.

Forgiveness is remembering the Divine birthright of peace, health and love in all. It takes remembering that it includes you. The Divine spark resides in you and neither blame nor shame will ever allow that light to shine, only keep your good blocked from you. Forgiveness often requires finding the source and releasing it through counseling, journaling, prayer, 12-Step work or many other wonderful tools for self exploration. Love yourself enough to release the pain of the past. Do not allow it to taint one more moment of today.

Patience

Patient is defined as:

1) bearing pains or trials calmly or without complaint

2) manifesting forbearance under provocation or strain

3) not hasty or impetuous

4) steadfast despite opposition, difficulty, or adversity

5) *a* : able or willing to bear —used with *of* ; *b* : susceptible, admitting

In this society of instant gratification, patience is rarely taught or cultivated. You can use the internet to listen to any song or answer any question in seconds. You can find and even order anything you want, but when it is all that easy, lasting contentment is rare. Patience is being still to trust and see. From that faith and wait comes anticipation and excitement. The child waiting to see what Santa Claus would bring would not be so enamored if it was every week.

Patience is remembering all things in life are not in your time, but Divinely timed. It is the understanding that your good can only and will certainly come to you. It is a certainty of a just outcome when you allow time to unfold.

My husband often calls me a brat, because I want what I want when I want it. He is right, there are times I all but stomp my feet. But, there have been many things in life I thought I wanted, but Divine knew better for me. I know everything happens for a reason, but I often want to know now. Rushing into a circumstance will not make the door of opportunity open quicker; actually it may push it closed. The more impatient and frustrated you are about what you do not have; the more you are attracting lack into your life.

Patience is resting into life and allowing God to be God. It is not expecting my way and the answers, but listening for the right questions and direction for your highest purpose in this life. It is a calm trust that allows for the beauty to unfold effortlessly. If you tried to make a rose bud bloom by peeling it open, you would kill it. In the same way, impatience chokes the joy out of today.

Happiness is not getting what you want, but wanting what you have. Part of that appreciation is the awareness of today's blessings, but the other half is the encouraging thought that even greater awaits you. Life is not about getting to the top of the mountain, but appreciating the view every step of the way. Too many parents work hard to provide, but miss out on the valuable connection of relationships because they are more focused on providing for than living in the moment with their children. Patience allows you to be present and content now.

Spirituality

Spirituality is defined as:

1) something that in ecclesiastical law belongs to the church or to a cleric as such

2) sensitivity or attachment to religious values

3) the quality or state of being spiritual

Spiritual is defined as:

1) of, relating to, consisting of, or affecting the spirit : incorporeal

2) *a* : of or relating to sacred matters; *b* : ecclesiastical rather than lay or temporal

3) concerned with religious values

4) related or joined in spirit

5) of or relating to supernatural beings or phenomena

You are an infinite spirit born into a physical body. Spirituality is the connection that reminds you of that spirit. It is the act of connecting with the Creator. Some people find it through nature, music, religion, prayer, meditation or community. Each person has their unique connection to Divine. Although some choose not to connect; any moment of awe and wonder is spiritual.

Spirituality can be one of the greatest tools to a peaceful and joyous life. It is the act of living through the soul, not the ego. It is experiencing emotionally, not factually. It is acknowledging the Divine spark within you and allowing it to ignite you from the inside. It is a peaceful resting into faith for no other reason than choice. It is comfortably embracing Father, Mother, God, Life through practices and understanding, by surrendering personal will for trust.

There are many religions; all are designed to bring you closer to the Infinite Power. All claim theirs is the only right way. I offer that there is no wrong way to pray. The connection with the Creator in any language, religion or practice deserves the highest possible respect. Just as five people would explain a story in a different way, there are many versions and stories of Divine. Respect all reverence for the Infinite Light. Another person's point of view in no way threatens your own, unless you lack faith in it. Knowing the Truth inside is so much more important than speaking it out loud. By trying to deny another's practices, it weakens your own connection. This Creator loved us so much, he gave us all free will; to believe or not. This same Maker gave us this beautiful planet to borrow. It gave no single person dominion or authority over anything, but their own experience. It is not important to convince or convert anyone, but yourself.

God is Love and any time you show love, kindness and compassion, your spirit is the extension of Divine. Conscious contact with Divine is spirituality at its pinnacle. It happens through being fully present and in loving service for Life. It is not a particular prayer or amount of time that makes you holy or devout, but the intent of your love behind each word or deed.

Faith

Faith is defined as:

1) *a* : allegiance to duty or a person : loyalty; *b (1)* : fidelity to one's promises *(2)* : sincerity of intentions

2) *a (1)* : belief and trust in and loyalty to God *(2)* : belief in the traditional doctrines of a religion

b (1) : firm belief in something for which there is no proof *(2)* : complete trust

3) something that is believed especially with strong conviction; *especially* : a system of religious beliefs

Faith is trusting and believing in what you cannot see or prove to be real. You use it every day, but some things are easier to believe in than others. When you stop at a red light, you have complete trust that it will change to green. Yet, when paused by sickness or a detour in life, people are often are shaken with doubt and fear. Faith is trusting in big and small things, because to the Universe, there is no big or small.

Faith is stepping back and not interrupting; allowing the Divine plan to manifest, but acting as guided to facilitate it. It is a comforting belief that dispels fear and doubt. Regardless of what you call the Creator, it is knowing that Infinite Source will provide the answers and means to sustain you; just as a small child depends on its parent. It is not prayer for your choice of good, but for God's highest good as and for you.

Faith is why we pray for somebody who is ill. It is as a child lovingly asking its parent for help. But, the gift of that trust is enlightening. It is uplifting to know you are not in this life alone. What a blessing to believe you are under the care, protection, guidance and love of a watchful Parent. If you ask any person with strong faith, they will easily tell you it is their greatest source of strength. You can see the light of faith, which resonates from the Divine, in their eyes and their actions. True faith is so much stronger than electrical or solar power; it is Eternal Divine power that does not wean in crisis. It is the Light that strengthens and carries you through any darkness.

Peace

Peace is defined as:

1) a state of tranquility or quiet: as

a : freedom from civil disturbance

b : a state of security or order within a community provided for by law or custom

2) freedom from disquieting or oppressive thoughts or emotions

3) harmony in personal relations

4) *a* : a state or period of mutual concord between governments

b : a pact or agreement to end hostilities between those who have been at war or in a state of enmity

5) used interjectionally to ask for silence or calm or as a greeting or farewell

Peace is an inner tranquility and an outer calm and stillness. It is a state of ease and grace in which life flows without force or stress. It is an effortless trusting in the next right thing. It is an innate trusting of Divine to direct and control life, while you intuitively are guided to whatever is next. It is allowing all aspects of life to harmoniously intermingle for the highest and best outcome.

When you are living your dharma, your soul is at peace. You are utilizing your gifts for the highest good for all. There is an inner fulfillment that comes from sharing your blessings with others. There is a sense of completeness and wholeness that is peaceful.

People often speak about world peace, which would mean an end to all war. While this is difficult to imagine at this time in history; it is a worthy ideal to empower through your personal thoughts, prayers, actions and words. Anything you believe can be achieved. Please hold to the goal of world peace to help this planet come together in freedom as the global neighbors and brothers and sisters of Divine. But, understand that the first step to that is maintaining a more tranquil mindset, your personal peace.

Gratitude

Grateful is defined as:

1) *a* : appreciative of benefits received; *b* : expressing gratitude <*grateful* thanks>

2) *a* : affording pleasure or contentment : pleasing; *b* : pleasing by reason of comfort supplied or discomfort alleviated

Gratitude is one of the fastest ways to get out of a bad mood or self pity. In any low moment, look at your blessings. There are so many in this world that do not have adequate food, shelter, clothing or even access to medical care. Many people you may know do not have friends or family. Many people will never walk, cannot see or listen to music. There are many nations where you cannot choose your religion or speak freely about government or even the condition of the world. So much of life is taken for granted.

A gratitude list is a great way to acknowledge your blessings. List everything you would miss if it were not there. Some examples the list could include: health, friends, parents (deceased or living), children, family, home, comfy bed, teachers, mentors, health, transportation, a job, your favorite tv show, movie, song, sunsets, vacations, holidays.... The list could go on forever. It could include anything you could say thank you for. If it has enhanced this lifetime for you, try to remember it. Understand in the light of all of your blessings, any particular circumstance or perceived problem in this moment will eventually pass.

Rhonda Byrne, the author of <u>The Secret</u>, in her books <u>The Power</u> and <u>The Magic</u>, goes into great detail of the many benefits and practices of growing conscious gratitude to transform your life. Her books can help you incorporate this valuable tool in daily life.

Happiness is truly wanting what you have, not getting what you want. That takes practice. Often, you will realize that some of the things you wanted would not have been best for you in the long run. An attitude of gratitude takes a combination of many of the other virtues in your tool kit. If you were raised and surrounded by negativity, your default will not naturally be gratitude. It is a conscious act to change your focus to see all that is in your beautiful picture of life. Before long, your picture will be missing less; you will realize how full your landscape truly is now.

Think of how much you love to help people who truly appreciate it. Your gratitude can not help but attract more to be grateful for and people to help. You need not align all of the pieces of the puzzle of our life. Sometimes, appreciating the parts you see can maintain the excitement to continue joyfully.

Awareness

Aware is defined as:

1) *archaic* : watchful, wary

2) having or showing realization, perception, or knowledge

There are many types of awareness. Each time you learn something new you grow. Every time you understand why something happens or does not, you are more capable to deal with life's twists and turns. Every experience and lesson changes you and you can never become less than you are in each moment. You will often learn more from disappointments than success and those lessons are priceless. Struggle is continuing to fight the Truth you know, as seen in addiction or unhealthy relationships.

To be aware or alert is to be truly present in this moment, which is all you will ever get. It is to use all of your senses to experience now to the fullest. It is only in this present moment that you have the ability to learn from any circumstance. Everything happens for a reason, if you are not present, you could miss the gift of the lesson. Time and experience often bring wisdom through these moments of truth. Once you have become enlightened by Truth, although life looks the same, the eyes it is seen through have changed.

Knowing the hole is there, does not always prevent you from tripping in it. In the same way, becoming aware does not automatically safeguard you from repeating a similar pattern that does not serve you.

The beauty in true awareness is that there are no mistakes. Each choice is a lesson. Each new day filled with new choices. Awareness allows you to choose your thoughts and actions consciously and wisely. Living in awareness requires you to be more than do.

Serenity

Serene is defined as:

1) *a* : clear and free of storms or unpleasant change; *b* : shining bright and steady

2) marked by or suggestive of utter calm and unruffled repose or quietude

Serenity is internal calm and stillness. It is a picture perfect lasting peace which permeates from the soul to all that you meet. It is a state of contentment with life and self. It is a quiet understanding of Life. It is the answered prayer of acceptance, courage and wisdom.

Serenity is exemplified in the wise, but silent monk. It is the grace of a swan on the unrippled lake. It is when you trust the soul's wisdom and the Divine plan to unfold. It is the release of all fear for tranquility and understanding. It is when you know, without doubt, that all is well.

Some people get glimpses of this peaceful calm, others live in it. It is a state of blissful allowing in each moment. Serenity requires releasing all fear, anger, resentment, sadness, remorse, guilt or sense of unworthiness. Picture a newborn child in restful sleep. That innocence and perfection is your true state. You were born with it and it can always be remembered. It takes fully releasing the hurts of the past for the joy and possibilities of today.

Closing Remarks

I realize that the questions I have asked throughout this book are often difficult and others seem easily answered, but who among us has never placed blame, anger or even rage rather than admitting to feeling powerless? Each of these tools are Divinely guided and practiced and the only possible deficiency is in not realizing them in your own life. These tools will help you to spend more time appreciating and recognizing the blessings in each day, rather than the apparent problems. They can remind you of what is truly important to you, not just what may be perceived in the moment.

I encourage you to cultivate each of these tools as part of your daily practices. You can not be in the state of true awareness of each without feeling better. At times the small shifts will seem immeasurable, but I promise you that if you practice even one of these per day, you will see your life improve exponentially in proportion to your time spent on them.

Another way to practice them is by sharing them with others. These gems are Divinely given jewels meant to be shared and appreciated. I encourage you to allow their magic to perform miracles in your life, as they have in mine. Your inner light- the Divine spark- can only grow when you share it with others. So, I invite you to the beauty of YOUR happily ever after!

Should you ever feel misaligned, please pick this book up again and either restart from the beginning or from whichever step or tool you may feel stuck on. Remember that as long as you are taking part in this precious adventure called life, you will never get it all done. Beauty is only found in each day's adventure, not the future.

I send you blessings and love on YOUR Journey of Happiness!

Gina

All definitions from the Tool Kit are excerpts from MerriamWebster.com.

10 Steps on YOUR Journey of Happiness

1) Start where you are.

2) Realize you deserve to be worthy.

3) Believe in yourself.

4) Joy is the only purpose of life.

5) Trust your internal (GPS) personal guidance system.

6) Move away from fear with each step.

7) Seek help if you get stuck or stumble.

8) Surround yourself with positive influences.

9) Never lose focus on your dreams.

10) Be open to even greater dreams.

Acknowledgments

I am so grateful for the many wonderful people I have met along my path. Some were teachers, speakers, authors, mentors and especially my family and friends. I am truly blessed with a wonderful marriage and beautiful children. Each relationship teaches me volumes about myself.

There has been so much wisdom and strength I am privileged to have been influenced by. I am eternally grateful to the people in my life and even more appreciative for my ever growing connection with Divine, which allows me to appreciate them.

Thank you for gracing me with the privilege of your attention. You are the reason this book was written. Please know, as I know, regardless of circumstance, you are never alone. I love and appreciate the blessing you are. Please visit me at the web site: YourJourneyTo Happiness.com

May this book help you on your personal *Journey to Happiness!*

Blessings and Love,

Gina

Suggested Reading List

I am greatly appreciative to the many authors whose insight and wisdom helps me through life.

Some life changing reading I strongly suggest:

The Bible

A Course in Miracles

Alcoholics Anonymous (regardless of if you have an addiction or not)

A Course in Weight Loss - Marianne Williamson

A Return to Love - Marianne Williamson

Conversations with God - Neale Donald Walsh

Excuses Be Gone - Wayne Dyer

The Law of Attraction - Esther and Jerry Hicks

The Life Visioning Process - Michael Bernard Beckwith

The Prayer of Jabez - Bruce Wilkinson

The Science of Mind - Ernest Holmes

The Secret - Rhonda Byrne

The Seven Spiritual Laws of Success - Deepak Chopra

Think and Grow Rich – Napoleon Hill

Until Today! - Iyanla Vanzant

You Can Heal Your Life - Louise L. Hay

Your Best Life Now - Joel Osteen

52 Weeks of Conscious Contact - Melody Beattie

_O_ – The Oprah Monthly Magazine

Your Journey to Happiness

This book will guide you on your path of self discovery. If you go through each chapter and honestly go through each exercise, I promise it will help you to:

- Greater appreciation for yourself.
- Release guilt and blame.
- Forgive yourself and others.
- Recognize the good in your life today.
- Set realistic goals you can and will achieve.
- Better balance all aspects of your life.
- Learn how to act vs. react to people and situations.
- Release stress and fear.
- Establish healthy relationships and boundaries.
- Utilize your internal guidance system- emotions and intuition.
- Control your thoughts to create the life you want.
- Live in awareness to harness the power of now.

All of these things are part of the ten steps in this book to take on your path to fulfillment and lasting happiness.

Enjoy every step because the joy is in the journey!

www.ingramcontent.com/pod-product-compliance
Lightning Source LLC
Chambersburg PA
CBHW060943040426
42445CB00011B/982

* 9 7 8 0 6 1 5 7 4 2 1 7 5 *